PUBLICATIONS OF THE DEPARTMENT OF
ROMANCE LANGUAGES

UNIVERSITY OF NORTH CAROLINA

General Editor: ALDO SCAGLIONE

Editorial Board: JUAN BAUTISTA AVALLE-ARCE, PABLO GIL CASADO, FRED M. CLARK, GEORGE BERNARD DANIEL, JANET W. DÍAZ, ALVA V. EBERSOLE, AUGUSTIN MAISSEN, EDWARD D. MONTGOMERY, FREDERICK W. VOGLER

NORTH CAROLINA STUDIES IN THE
ROMANCE LANGUAGES AND LITERATURES

ESSAYS; TEXTS, TEXTUAL STUDIES AND TRANSLATIONS; SYMPOSIA

Founder: URBAN TIGNER HOLMES

Editor: JUAN BAUTISTA AVALLE-ARCE
Associate Editor: FREDERICK W. VOGLER

Other publications of the Department:
Estudios de Hispanófila, Hispanófila, Romance Notes

Distributed by:

INTERNATIONAL SCHOLARLY BOOK SERVICE, INC.
P. O. BOX 4347
Portland, Oregon   97208
U. S. A.

NORTH CAROLINA STUDIES IN THE
ROMANCE LANGUAGES AND LITERATURES

Number 147

DISTANCE AND CONTROL IN *DON QUIXOTE:*

A STUDY IN NARRATIVE TECHNIQUE

DISTANCE AND CONTROL IN
DON QUIXOTE:
A STUDY IN NARRATIVE TECHNIQUE

BY

RUTH EL SAFFAR

CHAPEL HILL

NORTH CAROLINA STUDIES IN THE
ROMANCE LANGUAGES AND LITERATURES
U.N.C. DEPARTMENT OF ROMANCE LANGUAGES
1975

Library of Congress Cataloging in Publication Data

El Saffar, Ruth.
Distance and Control in *Don Quixote*.

(Publications of the Dept. of Romance Languages. North Carolina studies in the Romance languages and literatures, no. 147)

Bibliography: pp. 140-141.

1. Cervantes Saavedra, Miguel de, 1547-1616. Don Quixote. 2. Cervantes Saavedra, Miguel de, 1547-1616 — Technique. I. Title. II. Series: North Carolina studies in the Romance languages and literatures, no. 147.

PQ6353.S27   863'.3   74-17394

ISBN: 978-0-8078-9147-6

DEPÓSITO LEGAL: V. 4.071 - 1974

ARTES GRÁFICAS SOLER, S. A. — JÁVEA, 28 — VALENCIA (8) — 1974

TABLE OF CONTENTS

Pages

PREFACE 13

CHAPTER I. THE DYNAMICS OF CHARACTER-AUTHOR-READER INTERACTION IN *DON QUIXOTE*

1. General Considerations for *Don Quixote* as a Whole ... 15
2. The Prologue to Part I as Structural Analogue to the Novel 32
3. The Effects of Chapters 8 and 9 Part I on the Structuring of the Novel 38

CHAPTER II. THE INTERPOLATED STORIES IN PART I

1. Grisóstomo and Marcela 45
2. Cardenio and Dorotea 54
3. The *Curioso impertinente* 68
4. The Captive's Tale 79

CHAPTER III. FICTIONAL "DRAMAS" IN PART II

1. General Distinctions between Part I and Part II 82
2. Sancho 87
3. Sansón Carrasco 88
4. The Duke and Duchess 92
5. Cide Hamete 98
6. Don Antonio 103
7. Maese Pedro 104

CHAPTER IV. CIDE HAMETE: NARRATOR, CHARACTER, AND SPECTATOR

1. Author-Character-Reader, Within and Beyond *Don Quixote* 114
2. Cide Hamete as Judged by his Transmitters 119
3. Cide Hamete as Seen by Don Quixote and Sancho 124
4. Cide Hamete as He Presents Himself 127

BIBLIOGRAPHY 140

for Elias Rivers, in gratitude and admiration

...That the puppets themselves did not speak, I had already decided; that of themselves they did not move, I also conjectured: but then how came it all to be so pretty, and to look just as if they both spoke and moved of themselves; and where were the lights, and the people that managed the deception? These enigmas perplexed me the more, as I wished at once to be among the enchanters and the enchanted, at once to have a secret hand in the play, and to enjoy, as a looker-on, the pleasure of illusion.

Goethe, *Wilhelm Meister's Apprenticeship.*

PREFACE

It is not without apprehension that I entrust to "los brazos de la estampa" this humble essay on novelistic technique in *Don Quixote*. The study is by and large the work of my doctoral dissertation, nurtured in my graduate school years at Johns Hopkins under the kindly guidance of Elias Rivers some nine years ago. For seven years it lay in a veritable "cofre, consagrado y condenado al perpetuo silencio." Friendly assurances from colleagues encouraged me then to resurrect it and Professor Avalle-Arce generously agreed to have it published in the present series. It is hoped that the analysis presented here may still be of interest to students of Cervantes.

The study takes a detailed look at the fascinating interplay of the characters, authors, and readers who populate *Don Quixote* and whose image in the mirror, at the border of which Cide Hamete stands, reveals a fleeting glimpse of ourselves and Cervantes in the multi-layered fictional/real world he so masterfully constructed. Chapter I (part of which was published in *Modern Language Notes* in 1968) deals with the way the whole novel is built around the tri-partite nature of each character as he slides in and out of the roles of character, narrator, and spectator. The process is shown to be fundamental to Cervantes' approach to the writing of fiction and essential in understanding how his work is structured. Chapter II develops this point by showing how "fiction" and "life" are intertwined and symbiotically sustained by their mutual interpenetration in the interpolated stories of Part I. Chapter III contrasts the linear interinvolvement of fiction and reality in Part I with the superimposition of the two in Part II through an examination of the dramas invented and produced by some of its characters for the deception of others, most notably, Don Quixote and Sancho. Finally, in Chapter 4, a full analysis of Cide Hamete's role in the novel is carried out to show how he too reveals his three-dimensionality. The study shows that he, though at one remove from the world of Don Quixote and Sancho, is no less susceptible to the shifting roles of the characters within the novel and no less free from the strictures that limit their control over their lives.

This preface cannot end without an echo from Cervantes' prologue to Part I of *Don Quixote*. I must confess, but without his irony, that the reader will find in this book very few marginal notes or erudite references, and only the briefest list of critical works at the end. I offer the study as a contribution of limited pretensions, hoping only that it will provide some useful addition to the increasingly brilliant corpus of Cervantes criticism.

CHAPTER I

THE DYNAMICS OF CHARACTER-AUTHOR-READER INTERACTION IN *DON QUIXOTE*

1. *General Considerations for* Don Quixote *as a Whole*

Don Quixote, in addition to being a novel about a man who made himself a knight in imitation of the books of chivalry on which his imagination had thrived for many years, is a collection of short stories, poems, and literary and heroic discourses. Although Don Quixote and his squire Sancho Panza receive the greater share of their author's attention, puzzling, seemingly un-integrated episodes in the novel remain to be considered. Criticism of the interpolated stories of Part I began before Part II had even appeared, and Part II shows both implicitly and explicitly Cervantes' awareness of the problem of their relation to the story of Don Quixote. Don Quixote himself, of course, is most indignant when he discovers (II, 3) that many pages of the published history of his deeds fail to deal directly with his thoughts and actions, digressing to concern themselves with what is for him totally extraneous matter. Don Quixote's scribe, Cide Hamete, who has to take the blame for his "error," however, is not so certain that he was wrong in turning to topics not directly concerned with his main protagonist. In a well-known passage in Chapter 44 of Part II, he laments his restriction to his boring task of recording Don Quixote's deeds and asks to be praised for as much restraint as he has shown. While in Part II Cervantes does manage carefully to tie almost all the narrated action to the lives of Don Quixote and Sancho, the artistic validity of the interpolated stories of Part I has not thereby been totally negated. For in Part II as in Part I, there are numbers of characters who claim an interest independent of Don Quixote and Sancho, despite their apparent adhesion to the supposed main thread of the story. And, perhaps more importantly, the voice of the fictional scribe, Cide Hamete, is even more evident and persistent in Part II than it was in Part I.

Clearly, as most critics of *Don Quixote* agree, the deeds of Don Quixote and Sancho, despite Don Quixote's protestations, do not constitute the unifying factor of the novel. Exactly what Cervantes' intention was in writing *Don Quixote* has been the subject of most critical inquiries into the novel. There is a general agreement that the novel can at least partially be understood as a parody of the *libros de caballerías* so popular in the 16th century. Critics differ, however, on the degree of importance given to this aspect of the novel.[1] The parody brings a double vision to bear on Don Quixote's and Sancho's deeds which undermines their self-inflation to the degree that the reader's sophistication allows him to ally himself with the author's ironic view of his character. The author's parodic attitude does not entirely explain, however, the presence and function of the interpolated stories.

Other critical approaches to *Don Quixote* involve the exposure of various patterns, psychological, linguistic, formal, and philosophical, which reveal themselves as much in the interpolated material as in the central story.[2] Many

---

[1] A thoroughgoing analysis of *Don Quixote* as a parody on the "libros de caballerías" can be found in José F. Montesinos' article "Cervantes, antinovelista," *NRFH*, VII (1954), 499-514. A more recent and most useful discussion of the problem is Martín de Riquer's "Cervantes y la caballeresca," in *Suma cervantina* (London: Tamesis, 1973), pp. 273-292. See also bibliography, *ibid.*, p. 435.

[2] To list only a few of the most prominent examples of critical efforts to find such underlying unities see: René Girard, *Mensonge romantique et vérité romanesque*, Paris: Grasset, 1961; Marthe Robert, *L'Ancien et le nouveau (De "Don Quichotte" à Franz Kafka)*, Paris: Grasset, 1963; J. B. Avalle-Arce, "Conocimiento y vida en

of the critics who have focused on the problem of the unity of *Don Quixote* reject the interpolated stories as a mistake and as structurally un-integrated.[3]

Few critics until recently have dealt in detail with the manner in which *Don Quixote* is narrated.[4] Although the fictional narrator is a device common in the *libros de caballerías*, and therefore an element of the parody in *Don Quixote*, its use in the full elaboration of the novel cannot simply be explained in terms of that parody. The increasing frequency of Cide Hamete's appearances as the novel progresses justifies careful consideration of his role in the work. From Part I, Chapter 8, when the reader is first made

---

Cervantes," in *Deslindes Cervantinos*, Madrid: Edhigar, 1961; Américo Castro, *El pensamiento de Cervantes*, Madrid: Hernando, 1925; Leo Spitzer, "Linguistic Perspectivism in the *Don Quixote*," in *Linguistics and Literary History: Essays in Stylistics*, Princeton: Princeton University Press, 1948; and Joaquín Casalduero, *Sentido y forma del "Quijote,"* Madrid: Insula, 1966.

[3] In *El pensamiento de Cervantes*, pp. 121-123, Castro discusses the problem of the *Curioso impertinente*, listing both the adverse and favorable opinions of other critics with respect to its pertinence in the novel. Although his list is not complete, it serves to give some idea of the grounds on which the *Curioso* is accepted or rejected. Bruce Wardropper, in "The Pertinence of the *Curioso impertinente*," *PMLA*, LXXII (1957), 587-600, mentions later critical attitudes toward the interpolated story. Both Wardropper and Castro, however, count themselves among those who find the *Curioso* integrated thematically into the rest of the novel. J. B. Avalle-Arce, in "El curioso y el capitán" (*Deslindes*) relates two major interpolated stories in Part I to the problems of narrative technique raised by the novel as a whole. See also E. C. Riley, "Episodio, novela y aventura en *Don Quixote*," *Anales Cervantinos*, V (1955-56), pp. 209-230, and his "*Don Quijote*" in *Suma cervantina*, pp. 60-79; R. Immerwahr, "Structural Symmetry in the Episodic Narratives of *Don Quijote*, Part One," *Comparative Literature* X (1958), pp. 121-135; Julián Marías, "La pertinencia del *Curioso impertinente*," *Obras completas*, III (Madrid, 1959); and Joaquín Casalduero, "La lectura de *El curioso impertinente*," *Homenaje a Rodríguez-Moñino*, I (Madrid, 1966), pp. 83-90.

[4] Good studies can be found in E. C. Riley, *Cervantes's Theory of the Novel*, Oxford: Clarendon Press, 1962; in his "Narrative Points of View in *Don Quixote*," MLA Speech (unpublished), 1965; in George Haley's "The Narrator in *Don Quixote*: Maese Pedro's Puppet Show," *Modern Language Notes*, LXXX (1965), 145-165; and in Alban Forcione's *Cervantes, Aristotle, and the "Persiles,"* Princeton: The Princeton University Press, 1970.

aware of Cide Hamete's role as author of the history of Don Quixote, until the end of Part II, Cide Hamete darts in and out of the narrative to comment on Don Quixote or Sancho, to praise Don Quixote or to doubt him, to ask the muses for inspiration, or to complain about the difficulty of his task. The character of Cide Hamete emerges not only through his own comments, but through the comments, corrections, and criticisms of his readers and characters within the novel. He is, in addition to being the supposed author of *Don Quixote*, fully a character in his own right.

The use of a fictional author who is also a character is not unfamiliar to readers of Melville, or Conrad, or of picaresque, confessional, and autobiographical novels in which the main interest lies in the relationship between the narrator and his story. With so much post-Jamesian criticism being concerned with point of view, this relationship of author to character is especially familiar to twentieth-century critics of the novel. The assumption behind the concern with point of view is that the author must select a single perspective from which the action in his work is viewed. A novel is judged successful to the extent that the author's position is consistently sustained. Norman Friedman's analysis of levels of control that an author may be granted in presenting a story is weakened by the assumption that in order to be good, an author must be consistent to the point of view he selects. On this basis, he rejects *Don Quixote* as unsuccessful.[5]

Cide Hamete is a different kind of character altogether from Marlow or Ishmael, for he is both *sabio* and *historiador*, both omniscient and limited. Despite uncertainties about historical sources and many indications that Cide Hamete had no direct contact with his "historical" char-

---

[5] Norman Friedman, "Point of View in Fiction," *PMLA*, LXX (December, 1955), 1160-1184. "I have in mind here, for example, the obvious inconsistencies in the narrative of *Don Quixote* as well as the often burdensome references to Cid Hamet, the author of the 'original'." (Footnote 30, p. 1182.)

acters,[6] he is allowed intimate contact with them and even reports on the thoughts and feelings of his characters in their absolute solitude. That Cide Hamete could appear in the novel both as a character and as omniscient is what leads Norman Friedman to judge *Don Quixote* inconsistent.

The problem is that Cide Hamete represents a preoccupation on Cervantes' part not so much with the limitations of narrative perspective as with the problems of an author who must exist on two different temporal planes: that of his actual physical existence, and that of his projected, imagined story. Tristam Shandy gives perhaps the best-known expression of this dual dimension when he contrasts the amount of lived time the writing of his autobiography has taken with the period of time that work has covered.[7] Tristam Shandy, in fact, represents in extreme form the problem presented by Cide Hamete's appearance in *Don Quixote*. Like Cide Hamete, Tristam violates the verisimilitude of point of view, narrating events which under normal human limitations would be unknown to him. But as in *Don Quixote*, the principal concern is not with point of view as such, but with the dialectic between the consciousness of the narrator in his own lived time, and the objects external to him, belonging to a preterite time, which he must order and project. Sterne's novel represents the extreme toward which Cervantes' only tends. For Tristam's lack of success in ordering his material detracts from the intrinsic interest in the story itself and returns the reader's concern and awareness to the narrator whose subjective states of mind are exposed to him. Cide Hamete, though clearly concerned with the problem of vividly projecting his material, is much more successful in carrying his story through consecutively from beginning to end than is Tristam. The breaks in the story line, however, and the inclusion of apparently extraneous material, do testify to a creative spirit

---

[6] Elaboration of this point can be found in Chapter 4 of this study.
[7] Lawrence Sterne, *Tristam Shandy*, Book IV, Ch. 13.

tending toward uncontrolled writing for its own sake, against the restraints of coherence and intelligibility.

The ideal situation which both these novels suggest, but never achieve, would be one in which the writer's time and his character's time coincide. If the writer could actually become the subject about which he writes, there would be no more problems with ordering the work or presenting it truthfully and convincingly. The consciousness of the failure to unify the writer's time with his character's time produces an enhanced sensation of fragmentation, again more clearly seen in *Tristam Shandy*. Tristam presents as actually happening a series of scenes so chronologically scattered as to seem incoherent if not carefully studied. Between these momentary acts of authorial participation with past actions and the lives of other characters are equally scattered and seemingly incoherent comments from Tristam's own time and references to his epic situation.[8] Cide Hamete likewise produces a sense of instability of point of view, though much less startlingly. At times he seems to be following right upon Don Quixote's and Sancho's footsteps, allowing their actions to dictate his words. Suddenly, however, he will shift his position and reassert his fore-knowledge of the end and overall control by revealing something which no actual spectator could relate. The result is that the reader is successively drawn into the suspense and interest that the characters themselves provide and is wrenched away from them to an awareness of the pen which determines their every gesture. Neither the reader nor the author is allowed too long to identify himself with the will and activities of the characters.

The problem of the simultaneity of the deed and its writing is presented more or less explicitly in the character of Ginés de Pasamonte. Ginés is among those prisoners on

---

[8] Bertil Romberg, *Studies in the Narrative Technique of the First Person Novel*, Stockholm: Almquist and Wicksell, 1962. Romberg uses the term "epic situation," which I have borrowed here, to mean the time and place of the author as he is writing, as opposed to the time and place of the story about which he is writing.

their way to the galleys whom Don Quixote encounters in Chapter 22 of Part I. Ginés tells Don Quixote that he is in the process of writing an autobiography which he has not finished because his life is not finished. He does claim, however, that when published it will put *Lazarillo* and all other picaresque novels to shame. The obvious criticism of autobiographical novels implicit in this boast is that there is no natural stopping-point in life from which it is legitimate to turn and recreate artistically former actions. *Lazarillo* is artificial and inconclusive because the author-character's life as writer in the present moves on even as he is trying to capture the past, the totality eluding him despite his efforts.[8a] Ginés's solution, therefore, is to live and write about his life at the same time, continuing both activities until his death. The problem is still not solved, however, for no matter how closely the one activity follows the other, the two are mutually exclusive. The process of living is open-ended, no certain ends resulting from a given set of means. The writer, on the other hand, must work from the position of the end, turning on already accomplished events and ordering them according to a pattern not obvious at their beginning. The approach to simultaneity of word and deed is necessarily asymptotic, as Ginés's unfinishable book suggests. Ginés's appearance in Part II disguised as a puppeteer again serves to illustrate the problem of simultaneity. As puppeteer he shows at close range how his audience's interest can be drawn either to himself as manipulator or to the puppets as they act out their story, but not to both at the same time. He must step behind his puppet stage while the interest is focused there, although he is free at any point to pop up and make his own voice heard. His voice and interests, however, are never inter-

---

[8a] That this criticism applies much more accurately to Mateo Alemán's *Guzmán de Alfarache* is clear. Marcel Bataillon, in "Relaciones literarias," *Suma cervantina*, p. 227, goes so far as to say: "...esperábamos más bien 'mal año para *Guzmán de Alfarache*'" as he makes the point, in agreement with Américo Castro (in *Cervantes y los casticismos españoles* [Madrid-Barcelona, 1966]) that Cervantes' unnamed rival throughout *Don Quixote* I is Mateo Alemán.

changeable with those of the puppets, who must also claim their share of the attention. The alternation of focus between puppets and puppeteer parallels the alternation of focus throughout the book between Don Quixote and Cide Hamete.

The introduction of an author with clearly stated extra-artistic interests of his own reflects Cervantes' awareness of the fact that author and reader are still caught in an inexorable time process of their own, even while "suspended" in a work of art. The enchanted Durandarte's heart, although enchanted, must be salted in order not to putrify while being brought to Belerma (II, 23).[9] Sancho proves to his own satisfaction that his master is not, indeed, enchanted, in the cart which is returning him from his second *salida*, because he still must "hacer aguas menores y mayores" (I, 48). Neither art nor any other form of enchantment can capture life and suspend it motionless and removed from time. For Don Quixote, the most obstinate believer in enchantments and in the real existence of artistic creations of even the most fantastic dimensions, only confrontation with his own death will shake his desperately hopeful belief that as Don Quixote he could suspend himself in time.

Alonso Quijano's attempt to transform himself entirely into his self-invented character, Don Quixote, is as unsuccessful as Ginés de Pasamonte's attempt to unite his active self with his own analytical self-portrayal, and as unsuccessful as Cervantes' attempt to unite his self with any of his created characters. The scene of Don Quixote's penance in the mountains (I, 25) is enough to show that Alonso Quijano is not entirely absorbed into his character Don Quixote. For rather than spontaneously living an act of isolation and mortification for the sake of his lady, he sifts through a whole series of possible actions. He must choose

---

[9] Manuel Durán, in *La ambigüedad en el "Quijote,"* Xalapa, Mexico: Universidad Veracruzana, 1961, cites this episode in his section on the "Cueva de Montesinos" to illustrate Don Quixote's inability to escape the mundane and extra-poetic, even within the enchanted world controlled by Montesinos.

which, of the many models that his memory presents him, he must imitate. In such moments the distance between the controlling Alonso Quijano and his spontaneous, unconscious character can be clearly seen.[9a]

It is precisely this awareness of the inevitability of distance between the controller and the controlled that Cervantes has built into his novel at every level. And it is the underlying tension between the controller and the controlled that moves the novel forward and gives it life. All of the named characters in Don Quixote merit their presence there by their imaginative capacity and desire to involve themselves in make-believe or in artistic creations. They are irresistibly drawn to invent situations in which they can enjoy, and temporarily participate in, Don Quixote's madness. They happily give up their normal chores to participate as spectators in someone else's drama. They become narrators' telling the story of their own lives or that of others, relating excitedly a strange occurrence or a new turn of events. Their lives, as they appear in the novel, form a complex intertwining of imaginative involvement in a time and life other than their own with their continued actual existence. Although none is as confused as Don Quixote about where the boundaries between these two types of involvement lie, most of them at one time or another fall into the error of losing their consciousness of the separating distance. It will be clear again and again throughout the novel, in both the major and the minor characters, that a loss of the sense of distance between the imagined and the lived world results in a loss of that character's control over his own actions and over those of the characters about him.

Cide Hamete, therefore, as the fictional author of the whole series of plots and sub-plots, must be placed at a distance great enough from his characters to maintain a

---

[9a] J. B. Avalle-Arce, in "Don Quijote, o la vida como obra de arte," *Cuadernos hispanoamericanos* 242 (1970), pp. 247-80, and in "*Don Quijote*" in *Suma cervantina*, pp. 51-54, discusses the importance for Don Quixote and for the development of the novel, of this singular gratuitous act.

reasonably consistent illusion of control. The role of historian is perfectly suited to the establishment and maintenance of this sort of distance. For, in addition to removing Cide Hamete radically from the lived time of his characters, it implies the actual, if preterite, existence of those characters. The belief and interest in these characters establishes the polarities between which the novel can be said to create itself. In the case of *Don Quixote*, the characters' claim for the exclusive interest in the novel is especially strong. Not only does Cide Hamete affirm persistently the historical veracity of his tale, but Don Quixote himself affirms his own existence. As was noted earlier, Cide Hamete had to defend himself against his own characters' judgments as to his accuracy and concern over their thoughts and deeds.[10] Don Quixote's explicit insistence on being the exclusive focus of his author's interest is so strong that many readers, including some built into the novel, still take him to be the only important figure in the work.[11]

Despite the strength of Don Quixote's demand, Cide Hamete manages to claim enough of the reader's awareness to establish a feeling of distance between character and narrator. This is done in a number of ways. One of the major ways is by an arbitrary assertion of his control in stopping and starting his narrative. Raymond Willis' *The Phantom Chapters of the Quixote* shows how various chapter endings and beginnings reveal the hand of the narrator.[12] By ending a chapter in the middle of an episode or by referring the reader to the preceding or following chapter, the author intrudes on the story to remind the reader of his control and of the fact that the character is nothing more than words on the pages of a book. A more overt

---

[10] See especially II: 3, 4.

[11] Further development of this point can be found in Chapter 4. For a radical presentation of the position that Don Quixote deserves the exclusive interest of the reader despite the undermining efforts of his author, see Miguel de Unamuno, *Vida de don Quijote y Sancho*, 3rd ed. Madrid: Espasa-Calpe, 1938.

[12] Raymond Willis, *The Phantom Chapters of the Quixote*, New York: The Hispanic Institute, 1953.

device is for the fictional author to appear in his own voice to express the difficulties of describing a scene or character. Another common method is for the author to allow his character to dominate the scene entirely while he foregoes any claim to omniscience. Then, when the reader and author seem to be completely fused with the character, the author comes around and reasserts his complete awareness of the end.[13] Finally, the author can show his absolute control by including as much extraneous material as he chooses, relating it only slightly, if at all, to the actions of the main character.

Through a focusing on the function of the main fictional narrator, Cide Hamete, it is clear that it is not the character of Don Quixote, but the dialectic represented by the opposition of Don Quixote and Cide Hamete that forms the basis of the novel. An axis of control is drawn between the main character and the main author. The attention of the reader and the focus of the novel oscillates along this axis. Don Quixote is explicitly aware of his need for an author[14] and Cide Hamete makes it clear in his

---

[13] A good example of this was pointed out by E. C. Riley in his speech, "Narrative Points of View in Don Quixote," presented at the 1965 Modern Language Association meeting:

> The most elaborate case of gradual identification occurs at the meeting with the two student fencers in Chapter 19 (Part II)... We begin with the non-commital and ambivalent statement: 'Encontró con dos como clérigos o como estudiantes y con dos labradores que sobre cuatro bestias asnales venían caballeros. El uno de los estudiantes... traía, como en portamanteo, en un lienzo de bocací verde envuelto, al parecer, un poco de grana blanca' — and other things. Here the narrator has in fact all at once exercised his privilege to see inside the bundle; but the rest of the passage continues the process of gradual identification... The whole sequence is a remarkable example of narrative manipulation. The narrator proceeds at first as though he were as ignorant of the students' identities as were Quixote and Sancho on first acquaintance. Then he moves step by step towards identification, adding a little information from his own private store and letting the rest emerge from the dialogue. He participates in the everyday human mechanics of identifying strangers, but he simultaneously demonstrates the fact that he has no need to do so, and gives the game away near the start by looking into the bundle.

[14] Examples of Don Quixote's awareness of his author can be found in I: 2, 18, and 19; and in II: 3, among many other places.

famous final speech that he is aware of his need for Don Quixote. But though independence is an obvious aspect of opposition, so is dependence. It is in the striving towards, and away from, each other that the author and the character have created the work.

Seen in this light, *Don Quixote* is a beautifully unified work, in which the interpolated stories are as much a part of the structure as are the deeds of Don Quixote and Sancho. For while the interpolated stories can be considered externally as the expression of Cide Hamete's freedom from Don Quixote, they can also be explained in themselves as representations of the need for authorical distance. The interpolated stories are broadly considered here as all those narrations of plays presented or invented by some characters for the entertainment or deception of other characters within the novel. Basically, they fall into two categories: narrations to a surrounding company by one character concerning the narrator's own past and its relation to his present circumstances; and "dramas" invented and enacted by possibly two or more characters for the purpose of deceiving other characters concerning their understanding of actual events.[15] The two basic types of story reflect Cide Hamete's double role as both *historiador* and *sabio* with relation to the adventures of Don Quixote. The character-narrators are principally interested in relating a true account of past events, while the characters who serve as authors of the dramas are principally concerned with the control over other characters' actions and perceptions. In the one case it is the subject matter, and in the other the author's skill, which is given primary attention.

---

[15] The major exception to this schematic categorization of the interpolated stories is the *Curioso impertinente* itself, for its author remains unknown, never appearing within the novel to interact with the other characters. The audience to whom it is read, however, is staged, as are the responses to it by various of the listeners. The story itself, furthermore, represents an example of the second type of interpolated story; a "drama" invented and enacted by some characters for the deception of others living in the same temporal and spacial dimensions.

In both cases, however, the interpolated story is clearly set off, with the characters arranged according to their various roles as authors, spectators, or characters. By this temporary and artificial grouping a series of artistic distances is established which is essential to the production of the ensuing narrative or drama. In every instance, a narration by one of the characters is preceded by a description of the setting in which the narration is to take place, the appearance of the narrator, and the way in which his listeners are gathered around him. In this manner, the role of the characters with respect to the story about to be heard is made clear. It is also made clear that no narration takes place in a void. The story is the result of an interaction between interested spectators and a narrator with something to relate. Without both elements, the story would never take form. Although most of the interpolated narratives concern the narrator's own life story, all such narrators are suffering an unnatural suspension from their daily lives which gives them perspective. Their very presence in the mountains or in a roadside inn implies a distance from their normal center of activities. In these stories an external distance is supplied by the fact of the character's spatial remove from the events he narrates.

In the case of the dramas, the distance is more difficult to maintain because the actual and fictitious situations are temporally and spatially juxtaposed, and the roles of character, author, and spectator are not so clearly separable. In the dramas the distance must be maintained, though internalized, if any one character is to keep control. Such dramas as those enacted by Lucinda, Fernando and Cardenio in Cardenio's narrative, and Camila, Anselmo and Lotario in the *Curioso impertinente* show how quickly the artifice collapses when the characters lose a clear sense of the division between their pretended and their actual roles. In other dramas, such as those staged in Part II by the Duke and Duchess for Don Quixote's benefit, the separation between the artificial and actual worlds of the characters is more easily maintained. In all cases, however, involvement and distance are the omnipresent elements in the presentation of a fabricated work.

The combination of involvement in, and distance from, a work of art presented by or for the characters in the novel can also be illustrated from another perspective. None of the interpolated stories can be analyzed in isolation. Each narrator is also a character, existing and changing in the present. Just as Ginés de Pasamonte's life story cannot end until his life does, so the life stories of the narrators do not end with the end of their narrations. Although they are suspended temporarily from actual involvement in their stories, they are not entirely severed from their pasts. The series of love stories in Part I culminating in the final gathering in the inn [16] shows how the narrators' stories and dramas complement and affect their lived experiences. Cardenio is ignorant of the end of his story, but as a result of having told it, a situation arises through which he is able eventually to act out the story's denouement. The intertwining of narrative and lived experiences characterizing the above-mentioned series of chapters in Part I illustrates from the perspective of the reader how the two types of experiences are naturally integrated in every life. On this level the reader is allowed to see how spontaneously any character moves in and out of the roles of author, spectator and character, and in and out of lived and imagined time. The total character is revealed as the combination of all these roles and both these times. The same things can be said of the dramas, especially prominant in Part II. The major point in those cases, however, is that characters move as inevitably from the position of controller to that of controlled as the narrators move from imagined to lived time.

The interpolated stories allow the reader to see fictional narrators from a vantage point which reveals how the artis-

---

[16] I: 26-46. J. B. Avalle-Arce (*La novela pastoril española*, Madrid: Revista de Occidente, 1959) has an interesting analysis of the way this scene in the inn contrasts with the artificial resolution to love problems found in Jorge de Montemayor's *Diana* which was critized in Chapter 6 of Part I.

tic and non-artistic aspects of their lives intermingle. Because the reader is at two removes from the stories that the character-narrators tell, he can not only share the enjoyment of the character-spectators in the story told, but also observe as spectacle their reactions. The reader sees the interrelation between a series of stories, and the reactions, build-ups and after-effects of those stories. These effects are achieved sequentially, and as separate entities. Yet viewed from a distance and as a whole, certain patterns emerge to unify the seemingly separate story elements into a totality. The struggle to achieve simultaneity of author's and character's time, though impossible through the efforts of either of the principals in the opposition established, can be resolved at a distance. At a remove which transforms both character and author into characters, and fiction and real life into fiction, the amalgam produces an effect of unity rather than of unresolved oppositions. This phenomenon, so clearly demonstrable on the level of the interpolated stories, can now be seen to constitute the reason for Cide Hamete's appearance in the novel as fictional narrator.

The initial discovery as a result of which an inquiry was made into the structure of the interpolated stories was that the fictional narrator, Cide Hamete, claimed interest apart from Don Quixote and Sancho. The interpolated stories themselves seemed to be an expression of Cide Hamete's desire to free himself from the control of his main character. By his comments and complaints Cide Hamete established himself not simply as an impersonal scribe of someone else's history, but as a character independently interesting. The reader sees him as a character, however, not through his own comments alone. His work, as the reader discovers in Chapters 8 and 9 of Part I, has undergone two revisions by the time it becomes the novel *Don Quixote*. The translator and the so-called Second Author, through whom Cide Hamete's history is transmitted, see fit to include within the rewritten account of Don Quixote's deeds their own reactions to the story and its

Moorish author. By the ingenious touch of having the characters in Part II become aware both of the existence of a written history about them and of the author of that history, Cide Hamete and the story can be judged by his characters as well as by his readers. The result is the emergence of a pattern which exactly duplicates those more clearly seen in the interpolated stories. A narrator who is also a character tells a story for an audience without whom the story would not exist. The reader is allowed to see, therefore, both the story and the reaction it produces in its audience. He also sees how the characters in the story eventually appear to confirm on their own terms what has been told about them. The author is evidently responsible both to his audience and his characters, between whom he must balance their potentially opposing demands for a true and yet suspenseful story. The pattern of Cide Hamete's relationship to his characters and audience clearly duplicates the narrators' relationship to their characters and audience in the interpolated stories.

This would seem to be a work completely self-enclosed, with readers, authors, and characters built in at every level to move the story forward. The obvious fallacy, however, is that no author can also be a character externally viewed within his own story without relinquishing his ultimate authority. Just as the series of interpolated stories can only be fitted into an over-all pattern by a scribe whose distance allows him to interconnect the events meaningfully, so Cide Hamete's extraneous comments and the comments about him must be handled by someone external and distant from him. The translator and the Second Author fill this role almost entirely, but ultimately they, too, must have an author through whom they can be presented in the third person. The only appearance of this final, ultimate author is at the end of Chapter 8, Part I, where he appears to tie the end of the first part of the manuscript of the story to the Second Author, who immediately takes upon himself the responsibility of finding and transmitting the remainder.[17] In this single appearance, the author remains entirely anonymous, preferring the impersonal reflexive to any recourse to a first-person pronoun.

A novel constructed as a series of stories within stories necessarily suggests a vertical as well as a horizontal axis along which interest can be focused. In *Don Quixote*, each fictional narrator points beyond himself to another by whom he is controlled when he loses control of his own narrative or dramatic fabrication. As the interest moves upward along the scale of levels of fictional narrators, the balance of their dual roles as characters and authors moves more and more toward the authorial side of their character. The reader knows much less, for example, about Cide Hamete than he knows about the Duke and Duchess of Part II. On the other hand, he knows less about the translator and the Second Author than he does about Cide Hamete. About the ultimate author nothing is known. Awareness of his existence comes only by extension of the trajectory implied in the series leading from the character-authors to Cide Hamete to the translator to the Second Author.

The reason for this disappearance of the author behind a series of fictional authors should be clear from the various ways the problem of the relation of an author to his work has been built into the novel. The lesson repeated over and over again within the interpolated stories is that the fictional author controls the interests and actions of those around him so long as he can maintain a projected story or situation separate and clearly distinct from his actual situation. He becomes a character subject to the control of others the moment the awareness of the distinction between the story and the position of the story-teller breaks down in his mind. Distance is the prerequisite of artistic control, as both the horizontal and the vertical axes

---

[17] For good studies of this critical juncture in the novel see Haley, "The Narrator in *Don Quixote*: Maese Pedro's Puppet Show," *Modern Language Notes*, LXXX (1965), 145-165; and F. W. Locke, "El sabio encantador: The Author of *Don Quixote*," *Symposium*, XXIII (1969), 46-61.

of *Don Quixote* show. The seemingly autonomous nature of *Don Quixote*, therefore, is illusory. It is only the hidden, implied author who can be seen to have absolute artistic control. Only the entire novel, viewed as a whole, actually achieves the effect attempted by authors within the novel. Only *Don Quixote* manages to resolve the dialectic between character and authorial control. The resolution consists of a double victory: the novel can at the same time reveal the appearance of complete character autonomy, while allowing for the reader's awareness of its complete artistic unity.

2. *The Prologue to Part I as Structural Analogue to the Novel*

The Prologue to Part I, written after the first part of the novel had been completed, lends itself to an analysis which parallels the analysis of the whole novel at almost every point. Like any of the interpolated stories, the prologue begins with a direct address to an assumed audience. It is clear in the prologue, as it is elsewhere throughout the novel, that the reader or listener is the *sine qua non* of the presentation of the work. Although Cervantes admits explicitly to a concern with the response his readers will have to his prologue,[18] he also assures the reader that he is free to say and feel what he wants with respect to his novel. This same freedom of reaction is accorded to the spectators of the various interpolated stories. Every sort of reaction, from Don Quixote's excited distraction in Cardenio's story by the mention of *Amadís de Gaula* (I, 24), to the Canon's learned criticism of the pastoral and chivalric novels (I, 47, 48), is built into the body of the work. The readers of the prologue are beyond Cervantes' reach and their reactions are uncontrollable. Therefore, Cervantes simply abrogates any intention to coerce them to respond in a prescribed way. He insists on the independence of the

---

[18] "...¿Cómo queréis vos que no me tenga confuso el qué dirá el antiguo legislador que llaman vulgo...?" This and all subsequent quotations come from Cervantes' *Obras Completas*, ed. by Ángel Valbuena Prat, Madrid: Aguilar, 1962.

work from him and asks that the reader feel free to praise or criticize it as he sees fit. "Pero yo, que, aunque parezco padre, soy padrastro de Don Quijote, no quiero irme con la corriente del uso, ni suplicarte casi con lágrimas en los ojos, como otros hacen, lector carísimo, que perdones o disimules las faltas que en este mi hijo vieres, y ni eres su pariente ni su amigo, y tienes tu alma en tu cuerpo y tu libre albedrío como el más pintado, y estás en tu casa, donde eres señor della, como el rey de sus alcabalas, y sabes lo que comúnmente se dice, que debajo de mi manto, al rey mato. Todo lo cual te exenta y hace libre de todo respeto y obligación, y así, puedes decir de la historia todo aquello que te pareciere...."

Just as Cervantes wishes, in the first paragraphs of the prologue, to make clear the reader's independence from him, he also wishes to make the work he is introducing appear to be free from his control. Cervantes laments, in the prologue, the necessity for a prologue at all: "Sólo quisiera dártela monda y desnuda, sin el ornato de prólogo, ni de la innumerabilidad y catálogo de los acostumbrados sonetos, epigramas y elogios que al principio de los libros suelen ponerse." This statement reinforces the sense of the story's autonomy. It needs no preamble, no introduction, no famous names to justify it.

The relationship between distance and authorial control has been pointed out as essential to Cervantes' elaboration of his novel. Here, in the beginning of the prologue, is an explicit statement of this basic tenet. Critical judgment, he says, can only come from someone outside the creative process of the work. Since Cervantes clearly does not disclaim authorship of the novel, the statement can only be understood as a self-conscious attempt to divorce himself from the work while at the same time admitting his involvement in it. This process of simultaneously renouncing and admitting involvement in a story is the same as that which will be experienced by every fictional narrator and dramatist throughout the novel. The author must try, as Cervantes tries here by the use of the concept of stepfatherhood, to be both inside the work and outside it at the same time. He must have the objectivity of a reader as well as the ability to project the involvement of his characters.

The externalization of self implicit in the will to objectivity of the author, expresses itself more clearly in the second paragraph of the prologue. Beginning with a complaint about the difficulties he is suffering in the writing of a prologue, Cervantes transforms the prologue into a dialogue. In an instant, he is outside of himself, describing his own appearance and perplexity. From a general expression of difficulty in writing, he moves to a specific incident and situation. In the process of this movement from a direct address to the reader to a characterization of himself at a specific time and place, he has succeeded in separating himself from himself. Now he is both author and character, both involved and at a distance from the substance of the prologue. Again Cervantes has shown how self-exteriorization is basic to his art.

As author of this particular incident, Cervantes has the same advantages of omniscience that Cide Hamete will be shown to have in the novel. He has access both to his own thoughts and to those of the other character who appears on the scene to give him advice.[19] The story is dramatized so that the words of each character are transcribed, and their gestures are reported as well. Although the theoretical discussion about what properly constitutes a prologue makes up the main burden of the exchange, the dialogue is clearly to be enjoyed for its own sake, as this otherwise unnecessary description of the scene indicates. The mention of the interlocutor's gestures also provides a sense of actuality and verisimilitude to the conversation. Concern with the particulars of a scene, coupled with indications of omniscience, is characteristic of the manner in which the whole novel is presented.

---

[19] He says, for example, "...entró un amigo... el cual, *viéndome tan imaginativo*, me preguntó la causa..." (italics mine). The focus here is on the friend's view of him.

Another important factor in the comparison of the prologue to the novel as a whole is the way in which the matter presented duplicates the form in which it is presented. Just as *Don Quixote* can to some extent be considered a novel about the writing of novels, the prologue is a prologue about writing prologues. Not only does the author exteriorize himself, making himself a character in his own work, but he also exteriorized his problems as author, making them the subject of his work. The relationship between the opposing poles of author and character can now be more clearly seen. Cervantes shows in the prologue the process by which he distances himself from himself. In so doing, he objectifies himself as a puzzled, uncertain writer of prologues and converts this portrait of the writer and his problems into the very substance of his work. Without this self-objectification and presentation of his difficulties with the prologue, the prologue would presumably never exist. The very foundation of the creative act, therefore, must be embodied in this ability on the part of Cervantes to convert layers of himself into novelizable material in such a way that he can be his own author at the same time that he is his own character. The tension between character and author evident at every level in *Don Quixote* can be explained by the understanding the prologue provides of the creative process. The tension arises from the fact that author and subject matter are originally one. The distancing necessary for creation and control is an artificial one, difficult to maintain at all times.

The major spokesman in the dialogue which appears in the prologue is not Cervantes, but his interlocutor. It is the friend who resolves Cervantes' problem for him. This seems to indicate that however much distance the author may have achieved, the relationship between himself as author and himself as character is in itself unproductive. Once he has staged himself, however, he is free to introduce other characters who can open up avenues of action to which he alone had been apparently blind. The steady proliferation of characters throughout the novel reveals the same process at work there. Don Quixote cannot achieve knighthood without the appearance of others to perform for him acts which would be meaningless if he performed them for himself. The achievement of deeds of knightly valor requires other characters to present situations out of which adventures can spring. The presence of Cide Hamete implies the presence of a character about whom to write. No character is alone in *Don Quixote*, and no story is without its audience. This is the sense in which the novel appears to be self-propelled, for each situation brings about the necessity of the situations that follow. Cervantes' friend in the prologue, in the same way, appears in order to solve the problem of the writing of the prologue. He solves the problem as much by providing Cervantes with a character external to himself through whom to speak, as by the explicit solution he offers.

Finally, it should be pointed out, in drawing parallels between the prologue and the novel as a whole, that the friend's answer to Cervantes' problem is that he should imitate and plagiarize from bad prologues so that he will at least appear to be learned. The friend's discussion, in fact, is nothing more than a criticism of the typical inflated, pompous and irrelevant prologue and the manner in which such a prologue can be imitated. The prologue deals not only with how to write a prologue, but is an ironic treatment of previous prologues. This reflects the other major source of novelistic material in *Don Quixote*. For it too, while being a novel about writing novels, also bears within it as a basic element of its content, a parody on the bad taste of former books of its kind. An ironic distance from himself and from the works whose form he has chosen to imitate is at the heart of Cervantes' prologue as well as of his novel.

The development of the prologue is a perfect example of the way Cervantes expresses himself, transforming a basic idea of a work's independence from its author into a dialogue in which he, in caricature, reveals his self-doubt, and his friend ridicules the social customs out of which that self-doubt arises. Before Cervantes' pleas that his work be considered independent of him is an opening sentence asserting his identity to his main character.

> Desocupado lector. Sin juramento me podrás creer que quisiera que este libro, como hijo del entendimiento, fuera el más hermoso, el más gallardo y más discreto que pudiera imaginarse. Pero no he podido contravenir a la orden de naturaleza; que en ella cada cosa engendra su semejante. Y así, ¿qué podría engendrar el estéril y mal cultivado ingenio mío sino la historia de un hijo seco, avellanado, antojadizo y lleno de pensamientos varios y nunca imaginados....

The evasion of the narrator, that desire to establish his inconsequence as against the reality of the thing narrated, appears as characteristic of Cervantes in the only words he addresses directly to the reader. For the prologue can sustain only one paragraph in which the author directly addresses the reader and states the true relation of himself to his work and his sense of himself, before it falls into a series of evasions of its own. First Don Quixote is disowned, then the reader is set free, then Cervantes sets himself apart from himself and calls in another character to complete the self-presentation and the presentation of the work. The seriousness of the first paragraph dissolves just as fast into irony and burlesque, a tone which is carried through in the poems that precede and conclude the text of the novel itself.[19a]

The prologue to *Don Quixote* Part I traces the process through which Cervantes translates his thoughts into fiction, and the way in which he transforms himself into narrator and character. He becomes, in the prologue, the scribe of a conversation between himself and a friend. The work they produce together is itself a parody of a literary tradition. The concept of autonomy proclaimed for

---

[19a] For more discussion on Cervantes' attitude in the prologue and the meaning of the burlesque poems surrounding the text of *Don Quixote* I, see Américo Castro, "Los prólogos al *Quijote*," in *Hacia Cervantes* (Madrid, 1967).

his work reflects both the author's sense of alienation from the typical and his dependence on it. That is, like all parody, the prologue asserts its difference in relation to the thing rejected. *Don Quixote* will stand on its own, unlike the other stories. Cervantes will not plead for praise, unlike those other authors. The story will not be preceded by quotations and eulogies, unlike the other stories. The prologue, in fact, will not be like other prologues, for it will be a prologue against prologues. The autonomy is thus a sham in itself. It is flight from an established situation toward which it is at all times oriented. The oppositions throughout *Don Quixote* Part I are of a similar nature. Don Quixote is at the same time the creator of his scribe and the character with the greatest sense of dependence on him. The mutual dependence of Don Quixote and Sancho is well known. In a like fashion, Cervantes creates the friend in the prologue and yet it is the friend who resolves his problem for him. The role the narrator takes with respect to his character is similarly one of mutual dependence.

3. *The Effects of Chapters 8 and 9 Part I on the Structuring of the Novel*

The first eight chapters of *Don Quixote* are narrated by an author who occasionally refers to himself in the first person and whom the reader presumes to be Cervantes. At the end of the eighth chapter, however, when Don Quixote finds himself at the height of battle with the *vizcaíno*, this simple relationship between narrator and characters breaks down entirely. At this juncture it appears that there are at least two authors through whom the story of Don Quixote is being presented: one who has actually written about Don Quixote's deeds and one who is presenting this written account to the reader. Without even a break in the paragraph, the reader's focus is shifted from the scene of the battle to the manuscript on which the scene was recorded. The reader's attention moves from the problems of the main character to the problems of the author. Here the author appears for the first time as a character. He is presented in the third person and emerges because of his limitations: this author has called attention to himself not by his achievements but by his failure to continue. The reader is told that the author had excused himself because he could find no more written about the deeds of Don Quixote.

A new story is introduced at the end of Chapter 8, which, though part of the novel of *Don Quixote*, is completely extraneous to the history of Don Quixote's activities. Like all of the other apparently extraneous elements of *Don Quixote*, however, this story is full of thematic parallels which closely relate it to the rest of the work. The process by which the so-called Second Author is introduced takes place in exactly the manner in which Cervantes' "friend" appeared to him while he was trying to write the prologue. Here, at a point when the author of the history of Don Quixote has apparently reached a stalemate, being able to continue no further with his story, two authors appear where the reader had formerly believed there to be only one. The author of Don Quixote's deeds is no longer omniscient and all-controlling, but fallible and available to the reader. Above him, continuing the narration by presenting the crisis not of the hero, but of the book itself, is an unnamed author who disappears as quickly as he appears, leaving the task of telling the story of how the lost manuscript was recovered to a character whom he calls the Second Author. Clearly, Cervantes has, here as in the prologue, separated himself from himself, externalizing his role and problems as author and introducing other equally external characters through whom a solution to the problems posed can be found. The Second Author, like Cervantes' friend in the prologue, becomes the character who, taking over the role of author, moves the halted work out of its impasse.

The unnamed, controlling author, who makes his brief appearance at the end of Chapter 8, like Cervantes in the prologue, is privileged to an overview of the totality of the action that distinguishes him from the characters who must discover their answers in the process of the action's unfolding. He reveals this omniscience when he tells the reader, in the last sentence of Chapter 8, the outcome of the search which the Second Author will narrate at length in the following chapter.[20] The reader therefore knows ahead of time that the manuscript will be discovered, even though the Second Author describes later the dramatic sequence of chance happenings through which he found the story's continuation. This dual vision of discovery in process and foreknowledge of the end is necessary to every story teller. Cervantes makes this clear by having as the subject of his work the very presentation of the story. As with the prologue, he resorts to a dramatization of the difficulties of unfolding the story itself as a way of resolving the same difficulties. And here again the author presents his problems by dividing and dramatizing as separate elements the various roles an author must play in order to produce a work of art. The author must separate himself into two parts: one which will control the pattern of the whole, and one which will involve himself in the process of the forward movement of the story. The Second Author is the externalized expression of this second function.

The character of the Second Author parallels, in many ways, Don Quixote himself. Like Don Quixote, he is an avid reader who is fascinated with chivalric heroes, and disappointed when their adventures remain unfinished in the chronicles of their lives. Don Quixote, when faced with a situation similar to the Second Author's, reportedly reacted in a similar manner. The reader is told in Chapter I that when reading the unfinished *Historia de Belianís de Grecia*, "muchas veces le vino [a Don Quixote] deseo de tomar la pluma y darle fin al pie de la letra...."[21] The Second

---

[20] "...no se desesperó de hallar el fin desta apacible historia, el cual, siéndole el cielo favorable, le halló del modo que se contará en la segunda parte."

[21] Rodríguez Marín's note (Vol. I, p. 55 of the Clásicos Castellanos edition of *Don Quixote*, Madrid, 1964) is especially helpful in this context:

>Clemencín esclarece esta alusión del texto: Jerónimo Fernández, autor de la *Historia de Belianís de Grecia*, dice

Author, of all the readers of Don Quixote's deeds whose reactions are staged in the novel, is most sympathetic with the ambitions and intentions of the hero. He clearly believes in the historical existence of Don Quixote, and is as likely as Don Quixote himself to confuse historical with literary characters. It is his very credulity and involvement in the character of Don Quixote that makes him most likely actively to pursue the lost manuscript, for he has no doubts that the famous Don Quixote's records exist somewhere. Through a combination of his determination and a series of nearly impossible coincidences, he does succeed in finding the remainder of the story, which matches with the first part in almost every detail,[22] at the exact moment when it was suspended.

The other author, the one who disappeared at the end of Chapter 8 with the excuse that he had run out of material, is rediscovered and named in Chapter 9 as a result of the Second Author's efforts. In Chapter 9 the reader is introduced to Cide Hamete Benengeli, Moorish historian and author of the story of Don Quixote. Here, the reader first becomes aware of the possible conflicts in interest between character and author. The potential conflict is dramatized on many levels. Since the historian is a Moor, his interests can be assumed to be in possible disaccord

---

al concluirla que bien quisiera referir los sucesos que dejaba pendientes; 'mas el sabio Fristón (autor del original, según se supone), pasando de Grecia en Nubia, jura había perdido la historia, y así, la tornó a buscar. Yo (continúa Fernández) le he esperado, y no viene; y suplir yo con fingimientos a historia tan estimada sería agravio; y así, la dejaré en esta parte, dando licencia a cualquiera a cuyo poder viniere la otra parte, la ponga junto con ésta, porque yo quedo con harta pena y deseo de verla.'

[22] A number of problems remain, however, to perplex the reader. Sancho Panza, for example, is referred to as Sancho Zancas; and the marginal note which the translator finds by chance as he flips through the manuscript never again appears, when the manuscript is read consecutively. These minutia are insignificant in the light of the overwhelming similarities between the first and second manuscript, but they do serve to reinforce the doubts about the author's absolute control over his material which are suggested in so many ways throughout the novel.

with the Christian *hidalgo,* Don Quixote. His word can also be cast as of dubious veracity based on the commonly held opinion among Spaniards that Moors were liars. The Second Author exploits both of these ramifications of having a Moorish historian. He points out that it is "propio de los de aquella nación ser mentirosos" (I, 9); and that as natural enemies of Spain, authors of such a background might interject personal antipathies to belittle the great and heroic deeds of their Spanish characters. The Second Author closely identifies with Don Quixote and bears many similarities with the hero with whom he is so taken. He can therefore be considered a spokesman for the character's demand for autonomy against the controlling hand of the author. This takes its most explicit form in the final words of the Second Author before the recommencing of the story of Don Quixote: "... y si algo bueno en ella [la historia] faltare, para mí tengo que fué por culpa del galgo de su autor, antes que por falta del sujeto" (I, 9). Don Quixote and Cide Hamete are clearly mutually dependent, but at the same time they are independent characters, both of whom have significant characteristics through which the story may suffer modifications. The Second Author, both because of his spiritual alliance and sympathy for Don Quixote and because of his doubts about the historian's Moorish background, points out clearly the oppositions inherent in Don Quixote's and Cide Hamete's relationship.

From the manner in which the story was suspended at the end of Chapter 8 and from the parallels drawn between that situation and the prologue, it is clear that the Second Author is more than just a spokesman for the character's point of view against an untrustworthy author. He is also allied with Cervantes himself, as has been pointed out, and represents an aspect of his deliberate bifurcation. By linking the Second Author with both Don Quixote and Cervantes, the manner in which the author is related to the character can be seen more clearly. The Second Author represents that facet of the author's literary interest which associates itself exclusively with the viewpoint and concerns of the characters. Cide Hamete, on the other hand, represents the distance and over-all control which is the other side of the author's role. Cide Hamete eventually develops a personality of his own in which both sides of this opposition will again be apparent. But as he appears in Chapter 9, he serves the function, along with the Second Author, of allowing Cervantes to exteriorize the two constituting factors of his authorship.

The written manuscript would have been sold as junk paper in the market place in Toledo had it not been for the curiosity and determination of the Second Author. On the other hand, the curiosity of the Second Author would never have been aroused had it not been for the efforts of the historian, Cide Hamete, to record the deeds of Don Quixote. Here, the Second Author can be seen to be related to the third aspect necessary to the production of fiction: the reader. It has been shown, by parallels with the prologue and with the story of Don Quixote, how the Second Author reflects aspects of both author and character in the episode under consideration. By considering the role of the readers and spectators of the interpolated novels, the Second Author's relation to them can be seen also. In the case of Cardenio, for example, it is Don Quixote's interest and curiosity, sparked by hints of a strange man in seclusion in the mountains, that eventually causes the unveiling of the full story. In order to have the full unfolding of Grisóstomo's story, the spectators must make a special trip. The Captive, near the end of Part I, must be encouraged to tell his story by the group at the inn. In every case, the spectator must make an effort and show active interest in order to set a story into motion. It is the interaction of audience and author that produces the work of fiction. Both are essential in order for the work to appear. This is why no interpolated story is cast without its surrounding audience and why there is a constant shifting of focus throughout the novel from the story in question to the circumstances under which the story is being told.

In Chapters 8 and 9 of Part I the process foreshadows precisely the situation through which stories are told throughout the rest of the novel. An initial revelation of an interesting story is produced by a potential author. Some reader or spectator finds himself intrigued by what he has read or seen. He then must have the energy and interest to move the author to a continuation of the story begun. In this process the focus shifts from the story itself to the author and audience through whose combined efforts the story is produced. Once the audience-author relationship has been established, the focus can then properly return to the story. Even the story of Don Quixote is not free from an accompanying tale recounting the manner in which it is written and received.

Chapter II

INTERPOLATED STORIES IN PART I

1. *Grisóstomo and Marcela*

The story of Grisóstomo and Marcela is the first of a series of interpolated stories in Part I and reflects the same narrational technique as that analyzed with respect to the juncture of Chapters 8 and 9. Having seen Don Quixote as inventor and participator in the adventures at the first inn, with the windmills and with the Vizcaíno, the reader sees Don Quixote in Chapter 11 for the first time as listener, as the goatherds sing songs and begin, in Chapter 12, the extended narration of Grisóstomo's calamitous love. The setting for the goatherd's performance, although it is bucolic, does not correspond to the literary pastoral tradition. The goatherds who share their supper with Don Quixote, while enjoying a little burlesque poetry and song, are not idle courtiers in disguise, but actual herders of goats. This point is made several times, and serves to distinguish them from Don Quixote in their reaction to the Grisóstomo story.

The tale of unrequited love is introduced first by a messenger who announces the young man's death. One of the goatherds further develops the story for Don Quixote's benefit. Grisóstomo, as it becomes immediately apparent, shares a variety of traits with Don Quixote. Like Don Quixote, his actions appear to have been dictated by literary models. Grisóstomo was a student with an inclination for writing poetry. He completely renounced his inherited fortune to take up a pastoral life, tantalized by the elusive but beautiful shepherdess, Marcela. Like Don Quixote's chivalric ideal, the ideal of the feminine beauty and virtue that Marcela represents is literary and mythical, belonging to the same type of reality as that expounded by Don Quixote in his "golden age" speech before the astounded goatherds in Chapter 11. Don Quixote, being literary, imaginative, and idle like Grisóstomo, responds to the story in much the way that he must have responded to the books of chivalry. He shows great concern for and awareness of style and lexical matters, correcting Pedro, the narrator of the first portion of Grisóstomo's tale, to the point of irritation. On hearing of Grisóstomo's deeds Don Quixote resolves to imitate the poet-shepherd's despair over his lady's disdain by keeping vigil that night. His interest is enough aroused that he agrees to go the next day to see in fact the burial of him whose story he has heard. The others, though less literary, are not lacking in curiosity and also anticipate going to the funeral.

Pedro's part of the story is staged with both the spectators and the narrator forming an important part of the scene. Though annoyed with Don Quixote's interruptions — a theme which will become more explicit later — he does make the many lexical corrections Don Quixote suggests. Don Quixote's intervention provides an example of the way in which the spectators can be important in the narrator's presentation of a story. The narrator's awareness of the presence of his audience is a persistent theme in Cervantes' art.[1]

The audience's relation to the protagonist forms another important aspect of the elaboration of the Grisóstomo story. An interesting bit of news about another character can become a living part of an imaginative listener's world. It is the intrinsic interest of the story that moves the listeners

---

[1] The audiences's response was very much the concern of Renaissance literary critics. E. C. Riley (in *Cervantes's Theory of the Novel* [Oxford, 1962]), and Alban Forcione (in *Cervantes, Aristotle, and the "Persiles"* [Princeton, 1970]), both discuss this aspect of Cervantes' work in great detail.

to an action, which, inits turn, will generate further amplification of the original narration. The principal device by which the spectators are moved to action is the incomplete story, a device used at the end of chapter 8 to carry the entire novel forward.[2] In any story told, there is always much more that is left untold. Cervantes shows this structurally by building into every narrative in Part I a suspension of the denouement in order to reinforce the spectator's interest. In the story of Grisóstomo, Pedro ends his part by leaving the way open for much more to be said. When Don Quixote congratulates him on his narration he answers: " ¡Oh! aún no sé yo la mitad de los casos sucedidos a los amantes de Marcela; mas podría ser que mañana topásemos en el camino algún pastor que nos lo dijese..." (I, 12). In addition to providing the propelling force for the continued forward motion of the episode, Pedro's answer reveals differences in attitude between Don Quixote and the goatherd-narrator to the story related. For Don Quixote the tale is good and well-told and a delight in itself, not requiring further elaboration to be either appreciated or reconverted imaginatively into further adventuresome material. Don Quixote has already transformed it into literature and assimilated it into his own imaginative framework. For Pedro and the other goatherds, on the other hand, the story belongs to an actual situation with which they have long been familiar. Pedro's recount, for them, is interesting only as added information about a person whom they have known about for some time. This is a very small example of the varied interests a story can inspire in its listeners. Pedro's tale is a work of art in its own right to Don Quixote and a piece of news belonging to the real world to the goatherds.

---

[2] Raymond Willis' *The Phantom Chapters of the "Quixote"* (Hispanic Institute, New York, 1953), deals nicely with the problem of the tension built into the *Quixote* between spontaneous forward motion and the arbitrary startings and stoppings of artistic control. His study focuses on the chapter beginnings and endings as an example of this tension.

Pedro, by having the curiosity first to suggest that all go to the funeral and the skill then to tell Don Quixote what he knows of the story of Grisóstomo and Marcela, is the only one of the goatherds, except for Antonio, the poet and singer, important enough to be named. It is interesting to note that practically no character who is only character or only spectator is named in *Don Quixote*. They become important enough to enter the Cervantine world by name only if they participate imaginatively in the forward-moving process of the novel. Even characters who never actually appear on the stage occupied by Don Quixote and company engage in stories as poets or novelists. Creativity, imagination and curiosity seem to be the important ingredients in every truly Cervantine character.

A further comment must be made on the importance of the audience. Pedro and the goatherds all knew about Marcela and Grisóstomo. Had it not been for Don Quixote's questioning, the story would never have been told. Don Quixote's curiosity stimulated Pedro's narration. The awareness of the reader in the narrative process is a consideration of broad scope which will be taken up in detail later.

Here one can see, on a level that is less complicated, since it does not involve the reader directly, how intense the interplay of characters, authors and readers is in a world in which stories and real-life activities blend. Don Quixote is staged as spectator. The reader thus has an opportunity to watch him in the process of gathering into himself a character with whom he has only imaginative contact. He begins partially to incarnate Grisóstomo's passion by imitating, in sleepless imaginings, his devotions toward his lady. At the same time Grisóstomo's history leads Don Quixote out of himself towards the character who stimulated his imagination. Through Don Quixote's responses, the reader can see the story as a verbal masterpiece, a source for imitation, and an impulse to further action. The episode at the same time stands on its own, draws Don Quixote into himself through contemplation, and carries him beyond of himself through his search for its conclusion.

In this story, as in so many others to be examined, a narrator emerges from the same fictional plane as Don Quixote in response to a dramatic bit of news and the questioning of a spectator. This narrator reaches into historical data, orders it, and produces two characters who take on enough interest in their own right to inspire further contact with them. Finally, the narrator ends his tale leaving much to be said, and hoping himself to be able to discover further details. The role of authorship now shifts to another, who will be triggered into continuing the story by its intrinsic interest and the curiosity of his questioners. Curiosity moves Don Quixote, Pedro and the others to the source of the continued story and, from the other end, inspires someone to satisfy their interest.

Pedro leaves his story unfinished. In addition to maintaining the spectator's interest, this allows Pedro to move from the role of narrator to that of spectator. The incomplete story also rearranges the levels of fiction, making Pedro's recounting, rather than an entity in itself as Don Quixote tended to take it, a prelude — a prologue to a drama which all including Pedro will witness enacted before their own eyes. The Grisóstomo and Marcela, whose story has been told as history, can become living figures on the same plane of reality as Don Quixote and the goatherds. For this drama, Pedro has served as barker, drawing the attention of his spectators, awakening their interest, and then following them in to watch the characters, whom he had imaginatively projected, stage themselves.

In all the stories which are historically true within the context of the novel, the shift of a character from narrator to spectator is accompanied by a shift in the level on which the drama he was portraying is played. Thus, since Grisóstomo and Marcela are presented as historically real characters, Pedro becomes their spectator when they actually appear. This will be an important point to remember in contrast to the purely fictitious and invented tale of the *Curioso impertinente,* in which all characters, authors and spectators stay on their respective and clearly differentiated levels.

Between the telling of Grisóstomo's history and the scene of his funeral, the reader follows the characters' journey to the burial site. The spectators, in their ever-shifting roles, are as important to the novel as the drama they are traveling to see. Along the way Don Quixote's strange appearance and speech attract another of that gallery of Cervantine characters who enter into Don Quixote's world for being "muy discreta y de alegre condición" — a certain Vivaldo. Vivaldo's desire for entertainment and his apparently extensive knowledge of the novels of chivalry inspire him to engage Don Quixote in conversation, and to take an active role in carrying forward the drama staged at Grisóstomo's tomb.

When the spectators arrive at the burial site they find Grisóstomo in the casket with poems scattered about on his body. Ambrosio is acting as stage manager, in effect, for another play written by the dead Grisóstomo. After concerning himself with the final details, making clear that he has followed all of Grisóstomo's wishes, Ambrosio turns to the curious assembled and delivers an artificial, well-constructed panegyric. But even these two presentations — Grisóstomo's performance of his own burial and Ambrosio's speech — so apparently final and finished both in form and in substance, leave more to be said. Grisóstomo's body and his papers point beyond him to a single cause, the beautiful Marcela, the other principal in Pedro's story. Ambrosio's panegyric, however well-ordered, ends with a beginning: "cual lo pudieran mostrar bien esos papeles que estáis mirando si él no me hubiera mandado que los entregara al fuego..." (I, 13). Just as the forward progress of Don Quixote's activities threatened to be permanently halted by the loss of the manuscript, so the continued story of Grisóstomo and Marcela lies inert, remaining as nothing but papers in a coffin. The internal, creative energy has been replaced by sheets of paper, as easily burned as sold to junk dealers. The shell of the man and the shell of his creative effort lie lifeless before the eyes of the spectators.

The story has been told; the man is dead. But again the resources for salvation, if not of the man, at least of the written word, come from within the scene, and Vivaldo, of "discreta y alegre condición," moves in favor of continuing the life of these papers — transforming them again from their external emptiness to a living presence. Like the Second Author of *Don Quixote*, Vivaldo must use a bit of guile to reconvert these papers into imaginative material, snatching up quickly and without permission those which were closest to him. Fulfilling the same role as the Second Author, he transmits his finding to the audience which circles itself around him as he reads aloud Grisóstomo's last poem.

Here are all the devices analyzed with respect to the end of Chapter 8 and the beginning of Chapter 9: A story living in the imaginations of curious spectators who find the possible continuation of their story converted into mere scraps of paper about to be offered up to eternal forgetfulness; an especially curious spectator who is moved to save the papers from such fate; and an audience that reconvenes around him as he, having recovered them with a certain degree of desperate temerity, takes on the task of transmitting what he finds written to them. The similarities continue as Vivaldo, after having read the poem, is surprised to find certain discrepancies between it and the story as he had previously understood it. These differences, Ambrosio explains, are due to the particular situation of the author at the time they were written. And now it can be seen that, like Pedro's story, Grisóstomo's poem is also a prologue to some extent, intended to introduce the character Marcela, the subject of the poem. Ambrosio explains that Grisóstomo, being jealous, tended to berate the true goodness of Marcela. What Ambrosio says of Grisóstomo's authorship might very well be interchanged with what the Second Author says of Cide Hamete: "Y con esto queda en su punto la verdad que la fama pregona de la bondad de Marcela; a la cual,... la misma envidia ni debe ni puede ponerle falta alguna" (I, 14).

The differences in this handling of the continuation of a story and that at the end of Chapter 8 and beginning of Chapter 9 are also important to point out. For at the earlier juncture, the subject on either side of the drama of the lost and recovered manuscripts was Don Quixote; Don Quixote imperiled, but not dead. Following the interruption and the revelation of the functions of curiosity and chance in the propagation of the book, the story was resumed at the point where it had been discontinued. The only change was in the perspective of the reader who discovered that the drama of the continued existence of the book was as absorbing as any drama Don Quixote may provide. The loss of Grisóstomo's poem is far less consequential, of course, than the loss of the manuscript in Chapter 8, for it is at two removes from the reader, being staged not only for us, but for a company of goatherds as well. Furthermore, the recovery of Grisóstomo's papers can in no way add information about his fate, which has already clearly been determined. Rather than a circular movement returning the reader to the main character, the direction of the Grisóstomo story is linear. Each seeming stage of action converts itself with increasing drama and excitement into an antetheater which directs attention ultimately to the final and most dazzling act — the "maravillosa visión que improvisamente se les ofreció a los ojos" — the appearance of Marcela on the cliff above the sepulchre of Grisóstomo.

As in Chapters 8 and 9, the Grisóstomo story is carried by a series of narrators: first, by an anonymous messenger who inspires Pedro's story; then by Ambrosio, who produces the paper; then by Vivaldo, who reads it; and finally by Marcela herself. Each stage in this unfolding is treated as a story or a work of art in itself and all bear the marks of artistic ordering. Don Quixote congratulates Pedro on a well-told story, and Pedro counters by saying that more will come. Grisóstomo's funeral is carefully directed by Ambrosio, but his well-spoken panegyric contains the promise of more information. This funeral — in both the actual burial and the panegyric — is to the spectators the revelation of a story formerly considered a work of art.

Yet at the same time that it is "real" to the spectators, it is clearly contrived. While there is an apparent alternation between "fiction" and "reality," for the reader, at two removes from the action, all the elements in this story are bound together by an overall artistic control which converts what from the characters' point of view is a mixture of artistic and non-artistic events into a novel in which both are subject to authorial control. Grisóstomo's poem is a work of art in its own right but its variance with the historical truth of Marcela leaves still more to be said. When Marcela finally comes in what seems to be an almost miraculous appearance immediately after Grisóstomo's poem was read, she represents the dazzling culmination of an artistic process humbly begun as an after-dinner gossip session among goatherds in the mountains.

In a way both similar and dissimilar to the problem at Chapters 8 and 9, Cervantes has shown how art and life can combine in an integral whole. Each work of art is sparked by an actual event which in turn changes the course of events, moving them towards a re-crystalization in another work of art which produces yet another actual situation. The spectators in this story first hear about, then see Grisóstomo with their eyes. They then see his papers with their eyes and hear his poems. From the poems they hear about a Marcela whom they finally see in flesh and blood. It is now apparent that while on one level it seems miraculous that Marcela should appear at such an opportune moment, on another level the artistic ordering is such that her appearance is inevitable. For although creative interest on the part of the characters appears to move the story forward from episode to episode, from the vantage point of the completed series, the reader cannot but recognize the ultimate determining role of the unseen author. The actual appearance of Marcela, although indicated by all the previous stories and poems, was beyond the control of any one of the character-narrators, whose only recourses are to the imaginative or historical evocation of characters. The incarnation of their characters within their reality depends on a manipulator beyond their level.

2. Cardenio and Dorotea

The next interpolated tale in Part I, like the Grisóstomo story, is actually a cluster of episodes beginning with Cardenio and not really ending until the departure of all the characters from the inn in Chapter 46. In this collection of stories the intertwining of "fiction" and "reality," the joining of literature and life, and the intimate linking of the "historic" and the "poetic" reaches an intensity and variety only partially exploited in the series of literary fragments leading to the "miraculous" appearance of Marcela in Chapter 14. Far from being extraneous to the first part of *Don Quixote*, this series of interpolated stories is exemplary in the most profound sense of the word, for it exposes, on a level where the reader can see all the machinery, the very problematic of *Don Quixote* and of the whole novel.

The discovery by *Don Quixote* of letters and papers in a discarded bag in the mountains begins the longest series of interpolated stories in Part I. The written word is again the initial moving force as a result of which everything else follows as it does. The written word dependent, it must be added, on a reader to bring it to life. For the bag has lain untouched for six months, scrupulously left intact by the goatherds who did not want to interfere with the life of anyone else. Don Quixote, on the other hand, is driven by his curiosity to participate in the subjective view of another. It is this precise quality that he shares with all readers. Revealing the dialectic between literary object and living subject through which the entire novel takes form, it is Don Quixote who opens the bag and draws forth the papers from which Cardenio will eventually spring. Poetry, as any other literary form, points in two non-literary directions at once: backwards toward its author, and beyond itself to the external reality which inspired it. In the case of Grisóstomo's poetry, the poet and his fate were known, and the principal interest external to the poem was Marcela, the one who inspired them. In this case, however, the accompanying objects in the bag and the beautiful binding of the *libro de memorias* which Don Quixote finds tend to point Don Quixote's interest toward the author of the love poems he reads therein. Don Quixote's curiosity inspires him to find the author whose poetry and prose mark a man disappointed in love, and whose abandoned belongings in the wilderness suggest someone whose literary expression of disappointment is coupled with an actual lived response to it. The parallels to Don Quixote's situation are clear, as they were in Don Quixote's relation to Grisóstomo. Don Quixote would like to find the author of the poems he has discovered in the discarded bag. The chances of finding him being too slim, however, he gives up the reins to Rocinante, as he usually does when no particular adventure has drawn his imagination.

As was the case with the lost manuscript at the end of Chapter 8 and the beginning of Chapter 9, the continuation of the story of the author of the poems depends on more than a curious reader and inert literary material waiting to meet each other. One may move forward in search of the other, but it takes the hand of "fate" to actually bring them into contact. The same luck that brought the Second Author to the satchel of papers in the market place in Toledo now brings Don Quixote in closer to the still anonymous and disappointed lover of the *libro de memorias*. Scarcely has Don Quixote given the reins to Rocinante when he sees before him the fantastic figure of a nearly maked man leaping about the mountain side as if enchanted. Don Quixote correctly associates this strange vision with the author of the poems and resolves to search for him at all costs. At just this moment luck introduces him to a goatherd who reveals even more about the man whose traces have been so intriguing to Don Quixote. Finally, the goatherd's story finished and Don Quixote determined to find his man, Cardenio steps out from the thicket. Again the hand of "fate" has intervened at the moment when curiosity has reached its height.

A problem for realistic fiction is that at the same time that it must attempt in one way or another to imitate life in process, it must be ordered and sealed off at either end in a way which simply does not correspond to its unending forward movement. That Cervantes felt this problem acutely is clear in *Don Quixote*, for the tension between character and authorial control is built into the work at every level. The distinction, necessary to fiction, between lived time and fictionalized time, is made especially obvious at the end of Chapter 8, as has been discussed. The manner in which the characters' lived time and fictionalized time are intertwined can also be seen in the interpolated stories. By introducing literary artefacts such as sonnets, songs, and short stories, which have both the beginning and end necessary to a work of art but which are also linked on either side to an over-reaching story which includes them as part of their forward movement, Cervantes combines, in linear fashion, artistic ordering and the illusion of uninterrupted time. Here is Zeno's paradox contained within a work of art. Each of these various states of rest belongs at the same time to an over-arching continuum which has motion and direction.

Considered in other terms, in *Don Quixote* a distance typically separates a character-subject from an object which begins to interest him. Curiosity is the expression of a character-subject's desire to bridge that distance and to fuse as subject with outside material in such a way that at the same time, the object becomes lost in the subject and the subject in the object. This union cannot take place so long as the object is seen strictly from the outside as a series of fragments whose interconnection is arbitrary and unnecessary. In the case of Don Quixote and Cardenio, Don Quixote is the subject through whom the reader is brought into contact with Cardenio. Cardenio presents Don Quixote with a series of details suggesting a well-born young man disappointed in love: a bag in the wilderness, silk shirts, gold coins, a book of poetry — fragments which entice the curious to discover their unifying element in the subjective force that gives them a necessary interconnection. It is this process, by which a "curious" subject seeks to unite with and thereby unify inert matter, that makes Cervantes seem so often to interconnect the roles of spectator and author. Don Quixote can in this scene be taken as both "spectator" and "author" of the drama of Cardenio. He is a spectator inasmuch as his curiosity will not be satisfied until he finds the underlying unity of the fragments presented him, and he is "author" of Cardenio's story because, through his willful seeking out of Cardenio, Cardenio does eventually emerge as a subject. This is exactly the way in which the Second Author fused his role as reader with the role of author. For matter, whether it be in the form of an old bag, discarded paper, herds of sheep, windmills or a half-dressed madman, is always without meaning until brought to life by the will of a subject striving to reveal the object and to fuse himself to it, albeit temporarily.

Don Quixote's next vision of Cardenio is likewise fragmentary — the glimpse of a bounding man, half animal, yet somehow belonging to the same character to whom the bag belongs. For now a time-lapse has been suggested, and the goatherd's story confirms that six months have passed since the original "gentil hombre" secluded himself in the mountains. The goatherd's story, for all that it adds information, is equally unsatisfying, for his curiosity has not led him to seek out the underlying story. And, characteristically, Cervantes has not named this goatherd, for, like the messenger in the Grisóstomo story, he only relates the details he has seen and heard without having the imaginative involvement to seek out their essential interconnection.

The technique of accumulating fragmentary aspects of an object and presenting them to an imaginative subject is basic to Cervantes' novel. The technique produces two results: it shows how imagination seeks to convert scattered parts into a unified whole, and it reveals the limitations of fiction by constantly suggesting that beyond the boundaries of the fictitious world there is life so rich and varied that from within fiction it can only be glimpsed. Although some of Grisóstomo's poems were saved and read, most were burned. Don Quixote leafs through Cardenio's notebook and sees much written material out of which he selects only two pieces for the reader's (and for Sancho's) benefit. Both "living" characters and books, as was seen in the discussion of Don Quixote's relation to the book about him are at the same time subjects capable of moving those about them to action and thought, and objects presenting their exterior form as a series of unconnected elements. In the episode now under consideration, both the written word and the appearance of Cardenio are presented in portions which gradually direct us to a subject.

Cardenio, like Marcela, appears at the end of a series of allusions to him as if by miracle, for his appearance is beyond the control of Don Quixote, who is ultimately a mere spectator. The description of the meeting of Don Quixote and Cardenio is strangely moving, for it shows in still another way the intensity of Don Quixote's ability imaginatively to involve himself in the life of another. Don Quixote's relief and excitement on finding Cardenio are great: "... le fué a abrazar, y le tuvo un buen espacio estrechamente entre sus brazos, como si de luengos tiempos le hubiera conocido" (I, 23). It is as if in this action of embracing Cardenio he transfers the subjective, moving spirit from himself to Cardenio, for the next sentence shifts the point of view over to Cardenio and his reaction to the strange knight he sees before him: "El otro... le estuvo mirando, como que quería ver si le conocía; no menos admirado quizá de ver la figura, talle y armas de Don Quijote que Don Quijote lo estaba de verle a él."

After carefully selecting a grassy spot for the telling of his story and placing himself in the center of a group composed of Don Quixote, Sancho and the goatherd, Cardenio then projects a stage of his own on which he, his friend Fernando and his loved-one Lucinda are the major characters. The tale is essentially one of the eternal triangle in which one friend deceives the other in his desire for a woman loved by both. The story on this level bears many parallels to the story of Don Quixote's search for Cardenio. Fernando's curiosity having been fired by Cardenio's discussion of his love for Lucinda, he is treated to a series of fragmentary acquaintances, both visual and literary, of her. Cardenio points Lucinda out to Fernando at night where she is seen through a window by candle light. Fernando reads the letters exchanged between Cardenio and Lucinda. In fact, he finds a letter from Cardenio to Lucinda tucked between the pages of a chivalric novel. Through these tantalizing prods, Fernando is moved by a great desire to know more about the person evoked by this partial disclosure. He plans to confront and take possession of Lucinda. This drive, though expressed as love rather than as simple curiosity, is produced in Fernando in just the way Don Quixote's need to seek out Cardenio was stimulated. But whereas Don Quixote allowed "fate" to introduce him to Cardenio, and his curiosity was satisfied by hearing Cardenio tell his story, Fernando must resort to deceit for his fulfillment. He sends Cardenio away on a mission, falsely promising to ask for Lucinda's hand on his behalf. In a sense, then, he becomes the author of a "drama" in which the protagonists are unknowingly subject to his will. Fernando's curiosity grew as a result of a fragmentary vision of Lucinda, some of her written words, and Cardenio's praise of her. But unlike Don Quixote, he does not wait passively for the satisfaction of his interest, becoming instead the "author" of the artifice by which he intends to join himself to the one who has awakened his desires. His artifice is pure invention and he is the "artist" who orders the actions of the people around him against their wishes. This distinction between Don Quixote's and Fernando's methods of fulfilling their curiosity will be important in a later comparison of the *Curioso impertinente* to the Captive's story.

Although Cardenio had intended his story to be told fully and completely, Don Quixote's interruption halts progress at the point when Cardenio mentions *Amadís de Gaula* as the vehicle by which he was to send Lucinda a letter. The interruption, though caused by different circumstances than the one at the end of Chapter 8, serves the similar function of removing the reader's focus from one level of fiction to another, shifting the interest from Cardenio's story to his "lived" present with Don Quixote. Formerly in a narrator-audience relationship, the two now become characters, playing out a story narrated by Cide Hamete. But here a further twist is added. Cardenio, once the interruption has been made, moves from a state of sanity to insanity, just as the goatherd had warned that he was likely to. The result is the transposition of his real distress into a fictionalized one in which characters from *libros de caballerías* represent his tragedy. The well-ordered scene in which Cardenio was narrator and Don Quixote audience of a projected drama of deceit, has become a chaos of antagonism between the two as characters, both of whom imagine themselves to be active participants in the fictitious world of a chivalric novel in which Elisabat and Madásima are involved in an illicit affair. Clearly Cardenio's violence erupts as a result of his identification of Fernando and Lucinda with the two fictitious characters. And clearly Don Quixote defends Madásima's honor because he defends ladies' honor on principle, whether they be "fictitious" or "real." The conflict could appear to be a lapse into madness by Cardenio and Don Quixote and totally unrelated to the actual unfolding of Cardenio's story. The fact is, however, that just as their actual situations lead them to this absurd flight of fancy, so this flight of fancy will participate in the subsequent unfolding of the story. None of these incidents, however apparently removed from the "true" story, is actually extraneous. The point at which Cardenio's story was interrupted left the reader unaware of the outcome of Fernando's guile. Cardenio's leap into fantasy and his accusation of Madásima project the outcome from Cardenio's point of view ahead in time. On reading the entire episode the reader discovers that Don Quixote's defense of Madásima is also related to the final denouement. In time, in process, each of these particles appears to be a disconnected fragment. But when the reader has achieved the distance from which he can view the overarching trajectory of the story, be can see that each piece, whether "fantastic" or "realistic," is knit into the main line of the story.

When Cardenio next appears, his spectators are the Curate and the Barber, who already know about Cardenio from Sancho. In the same way as Don Quixote, the Barber and Curate are drawn to Cardenio by a series of artistic and visual glimpses, since they first hear him singing his own poetry and then see him in strange apparel. The Curate and the Barber, who in the *escrutinio* showed a reasonable sense of discrimination between "poetry" and "truth," are on a mission to save Don Quixote from erroneously trying to live in a world that belongs only to books. They find themselves, however, confronted with an actual situation that seems to correspond to what they had thought could only be found in pastoral novels: "Estando, pues, los dos allí, sosegados y a la sombra, llegó a sus oídos una voz que, sin acompañarla son de algún instrumento, dulce y regaladamente sonaba, de que no poco se admiraron, por parecerles que aquél no era lugar donde pudiese haber quien tan bien cantase. Porque, aunque suele decirse que por las selvas y campos se hallan pastores de voces extremadas, más son encarecimientos de poetas que verdades..." (I, 27). These solid citizens of the "real" world, it seems, are likely to be as wrong in assuming there is no relation between art and life as Don Quixote is wrong in identifying the two. Despite their surprise, they seek Cardenio out, moved by his poetry and song, and become the new audience for his continued story.

Again, however, the story is left unended, this time not by the interruption of the audience, but by Cardenio's own interruption, from within his story, of the "drama" of which he had been a spectator. Fernando's artifice, dealing as it did with characters on the same level of reality as himself, made necessary a counter-plot by Lucinda in which she would be main actress and Cardenio would be the very involved spectator. In this counter-plot the setting is the same as for Fernando's "play": the wedding. At the final moment Lucinda had promised Cardenio to say "no" rather than "*sí*" to the question of whether she would marry Fernando, eluding at that point the controlling net which Fernando, by his guile, had tried to place over her. In this scene the inter-involvements are so great that the separation between spectator, character and author is ready to explode at any minute into an actual chaos. When Lucinda finally whispers the words Fernando, rather than Cardenio, had expected her to say, the tenuous ordering breaks down into a disorder whose effects are still evident in Cardenio. Very like Don Quixote in the previous scene, Cardenio allows his own eagerness and involvement as spectator to interrupt the drama before it ended.

No sooner has Cardenio finished his unfinished story than, in an almost identical way to that by which they found Cardenio, the Curate and the Barber find Dorotea. Urged to tell her story, she begins revealing by degrees to Cardenio that the story which he had just been narrating links itself not only with Dorotea's own disappointment in love, but with his own story at the point that he had lost knowledge of it.

In the Grisóstomo episode, Marcela herself appeared, having been evoked by a series of references to her. In this story, Dorotea does not emerge as an embodiment of a previous evocation of her, for her name has never been mentioned before. The readers are as ignorant as Cardenio, the Curate and the Barber are of her existence. Here the miraculous appearance takes place on the stage which Cardenio has left in chaos. For Dorotea, out of nowhere, tells a story which reopens the curtains on the scene which Cardenio had been narrating. Dorotea's story has the same characters, whose action, no longer suspended at the moment when Lucinda appears to agree to marry Fernando, is allowed to continue. The ex-narrator Cardenio watches in amazement as his own story unfolds before him, finishing up the scene which he had left in confusion and desperation. At the end of Chapter 8, also, the author had to leave the audience uncertain of his character's fate for lack of further knowledge. There chance and a curious spectator combined to move the story out of its impasse. Here, where curiosity is at its most intense, and spectator involvement is total and vital, only the intervention of fate can bring the story forward.

As Dorotea's story progresses, she adds name after familiar name to the list of people she is "staging," and

Cardenio finds it harder and harder to remain a spectator to her tale ("Cuando Cardenio le oyó decir que se llamaba Dorotea, tornó de nuevo a sus sobresaltos y acabó de confirmar por verdadera su primera opinión; pero no quiso interrumpir el cuento, por ver en qué venía a parar lo que él casi sabía" [I, 28]). He can restrain his impulse to break out of his role as spectator in Dorotea's story, however, because of his distance from the narrated scene. When he was spectator of the "play" which was being acted out on the same level of reality as his own life, the tension between his artificial role as spectator and his "real" role as lover was too great to bear the burden of his loved-one's seeming desertion of him. Now, however, he and Dorotea are at one remove from the "drama." No matter how intense his involvement may still be, as he sees himself and his fate unfold in the story he is listening to, Cardenio can now avoid interrupting the forward motion of the story.

Cardenio and Dorotea, like Grisóstomo in the previous story, have lived disguised and in isolation, lamenting their misfortunes in love. But their involvement with the stories they narrate is far more complicated than Grisóstomo's for two reasons. Each tells the story of his life and must therefore hold himself apart from his own history. Cardenio's intermittent madness is the result of his inability at all times to maintain the distance necessary to narrate and listen to his own story. Unlike Grisóstomo, Cardenio and Dorotea must be both the narrators and the main characters of their stories. Implicit in the first reason, Cardenio's and Dorotea's stories differ from Grisóstomo's in that their fates are still undecided, for no character can tell the completed story of his own life. In the Grisóstomo story, the presence of first the dead Grisóstomo and then the living Marcela verified the tale of them told by Pedro. In the present case, however, the verification for Cardenio's narration is not his actual "flesh and blood" presence, nor is it Dorotea's (for she is never named by Cardenio). Rather, the verification takes place on the level of the story Cardenio tells, by its perfect joining with Dorotea's. The relationship between Cardenio's and Dorotea's present, lived time and the time of their narrations is extremely complex, as is inevitable in any autobiographical or confessional work. The complications result from the fact that the epic situation of the character-narrators is an artificial state directly related to the past situation which they are narrating. It is only from their positions of suspension from direct involvement in the "drama" they tell that they have the distance necessary for their narrations. On the other hand, it is the unfortunate outcome of the "drama" itself which has caused them to be in their present situation. Both the unnatural situation from which Cardenio and Dorotea speak and the drama they narrate are left unresolved. Only an unexpected denouement to the drama can cause the reintegration of the narrators into the normal course of their lives.

While they are controlling the story they are telling to Don Quixote and the others, the story they tell is actually controlling them. This is why in Cervantes there is a criticism of the autobiographical picaresque novel. An author can only control a subject on which he has enough distance to not be dependent on any of the characters in the story he narrates. He must also have a distance which allows a previous awareness of the end. Cardenio and Dorotea are perfect examples of the problems inherent in first-person narrations. In the case of Dorotea and Cardenio, their present rustic disguise is dependent upon Fernando's deception. Dorotea and Cardenio appear to be narrators, on the same plane of reality as the Curate and the Barber, of a story in which they and Fernando are at one remove as characters. In fact, however, Fernando, who is a principal character in both Dorotea's and Cardenio's narrations, is actually "author" of a "drama" in which Cardenio and Dorotea are characters. It is his deceit and intransigence that caused them to escape to the wilderness in the guise of shepherds. The resolution of their present state will depend upon Fernando's word. Dorotea and Cardenio only recognize each other with relation to their roles in the stories both have told. Here, their "fiction" — the stories they narrate — is more "real" than their flesh and blood appearance as they tell their stories.

That the authors would be controlled by a character in the story they are telling seems difficult to believe. The Curate and the Barber, in fact, have shown us clearly that "stories" are one thing and "life" is something quite different. They are seeking out Don Quixote, at the moment when they meet Dorotea and Cardenio, to try to make him see that he is mistaken in trying to live a life drawn from chivalric novels. But here are Dorotea and Cardenio, embodying a "fictious" pastoral setting and telling stories more "real" than their present appearance.

Neither Dorotea's nor Cardenio's story can be finished. But in their cases the suspended denouement is not an artificial device used to intensify the suspense of their listeners. Their stories relate to a specific incident with respect to which they are as much spectators and characters as narrators. Like Cide Hamete himself, they are simply relating a story over which they have no control except in their choice of words and manner of relating it. But since the story they tell involves them directly, the solution to their present situation and the outcome of their story are very much interrelated.

"Fiction" and "reality" co-exist in Dorotea and Cardenio on two planes. They, along with the Curate, the Barber and Don Quixote, appear as characters "living" on the same level. In distinction to the Curate and the Barber, however, they are also "fictitious" (aside from the fact that they are found in a novel we are reading) in that they are playing a role which does not correspond to the one into which they were brought up, but which, rather, is patterned after pastoral novels. In this latter sense, they are related to Don Quixote, living, as he does, a disguise which isolates them from every-day life. On the plane of the story they tell, likewise, "fiction" and "reality" co-exist. Fernando, Lucinda, Cardenio and Dorotea actually existed on that plane as living, moving characters. But the treachery of Fernando transformed their roles on that plane in such a way that their actions and stagings were artificial, being directed not by their actual intentions, but by Fernando's manipulations. Furthermore, artifice and reality combine on this second plane from the point of view of their audience, for the stories told by Dorotea and Cardenio both are ordered, arranged works of art and relate to a true situation.

Still another level on which "truth" and "fiction" coexist is introduced by the joining together of the Curate and the Barber, Dorotea and Cardenio, on a single plane of action. Cardenio and Dorotea, unlike Don Quixote, are in their present disguise against their will. The direction in which they wish to move is not linear but circular, as both live with the hope of returning to their "pre-historic" state. The completion of their return is prepared by their discovery of one another, for with both sharing the same story, they are no longer isolated *locos*, but show that they are capable of social contact with others on their same level. The four, then, can represent a "truth" by contrast with which Don Quixote is living a "fiction." The four collaborate from this basis to create a drama in which Don Quixote can participate as character. In this drama the Curate serves as "author," having planned the manner in which the artifice will attract Don Quixote's imagination, and as spectator, declining to disguise himself as a maiden and assigning the part ultimately to Dorotea. Dorotea, having been told the basic outline of her role and given a fictitious name and origin by the Curate, is launched onto the scene with Don Quixote, and draws from her own imagination the words and actions which conform to a lady in distress in a chivalric novel. Throughout her presentation the Curate serves as prompter as well as spectator to a play which he has set into motion, and can now enjoy. But Dorotea's story, though fictitious, relates directly to her real distress. The Princess Micomicona, alone and wandering, is threatened by a giant who will leave her forever homeless and dishonored unless killed. Her pretense with respect to Don Quixote is that he can help her by killing the giant. All but Don Quixote and Sancho are highly amused by her artifice and feel content with the way their imaginations have allowed them to control Don Quixote's actions.

What the inventing characters do not know is that by creating this figure of the Princess Micomicona they are being controlled by Don Quixote as much as they are controlling him. They do not know that Don Quixote has woven for Sancho a fantastic story in Chapter 21 in which he tells how a knight can become the hero for a princess whose father then gives him a share in his kingdom and the hand of the princess in marriage. And suddenly, here are Sancho and Don Quixote listening to a princess telling Don Quixote: "...mi buen padre... dejó dicho... que si este caballero de la profecía, después de haber degollado al gigante, quisiese casarse conmigo, que yo me otorgase luego sin réplica alguna por su legítima esposa, y le diese la posesión de mi reino, junto con la de mi persona" (I, 30). It seems that in this world of *Don Quixote*, two independently imagined stories can complement each other as easily as two independently narrated stories of a "true" event. It was already just short of miraculous that Dorotea's story should join itself so perfectly to Cardenio's. But, however amazing that they should find each other, the stories did correspond to an "actual" situation, and their linking in such a strange place was at least possible. Here, however, two entirely fantastic and fictious creations with no necessary connection with reality have met and joined in confirmation of each other.

The Princess Micomicona's story can be divided into two aspects. One, essentially "true," which relates in form to Dorotea's actual situation, and the other, apparently untrue, which nonetheless relates in detail to a situation imagined by Don Quixote. To see this double connection is very important for an understanding of the order of events in the inn leading up to the denouement of Dorotea's and Cardenio's story. The final rejoining of Dorotea and Cardenio with their loved ones follows Don Quixote's assault and imaginary killing of the giant whom Dorotea has commissioned him to overcome as a necessary pre-condition to her salvation. These are simply more examples of the fact that no character in this story by Cervantes has absolute control over any other character on his same level of "reality," nor does any character have absolute possession of the truth.

3. The *Curioso impertinente*

In the preceding analyses of the interpolated stories of Part I, the main consideration has been the distance of the narrator from the characters whose story he tells. In the story of Grisóstomo and Marcela, Pedro's narration, while holding Grisóstomo and Marcela at a level once removed from his audience, was "historically" accurate and could serve not only as a story but as a prelude to their actual appearance later. Their later appearance, in turn, verified the story Pedro told. Pedro was in no direct way involved in real life with the characters of whom he spoke. His story made perfect "history," for his attitude toward Grisóstomo and Marcela was interested but dispassionate, and the information he related was "true," as their later appearance and words showed. The narrative situation in Cardenio and Dorotea's story is more complicated because while "historically" accurate, it involved the narrators' own lives. The involvement of the narrators with their story was so intense, in fact, that their stories revealed their total dependence on the activities of one of their characters. Pedro, in the course of the Grisóstomo story, was first narrator and later spectator. Cardenio's and Dorotea's stories, on the other hand, showed how they could be simultaneously narrators of and characters in the story they were narrating. Whatever their differences, both of these first two interpolated story groups share the characteristics of being "historically" true and belonging to a world in which characters can shift their roles and become authors and spectators.

The major implication of a story's being "historically" true is that the levels of fiction can shift. Characters who at one point are encased in the words and the organizing imagination of a narrator can at any moment step out of those words and become "real" and of flesh and blood to the former narrator and audience. This shift of levels towards the reader tends to suggest confirmation of a story, emphasizing the truth of a former story. These characters, once they have emerged in person, are then able, in a more obvious and effective way, to interact with their former audience to affect their "real" lives as well as their imaginations. In this sort of world, where the levels of fiction are fluid, the roles of the characters can shift from narrator to spectator to character. This procedure strengthens the illusion of real life in *Don Quixote* by corresponding, simply, to the natural way that people interact.

All of this only reinforces the importance of Chapters 8 y 9. There for the first and really only significant time in Part I the reader is introduced to a narrator who stands between him and the world about which he is reading. If this story were true, like the interpolated ones so far discussed, the characters should be able to have the same mobility as Grisóstomo, Marcela, Fernando, and the others. Don Quixote, the Curate and the Barber, on the standard set up by Grisóstomo and Marcela, should be able to step out of their story framework and into flesh and blood concourse with Cide Hamete, or Cide Hamete should be able to move out of his level into direct confrontation with us.[2] The reason they do not, of course, is that they either lived in another time from Cide Hamete, or never existed at all. In either event, the historical truth of their existence is unverifiable.

Recalling the process of the rediscovery of the story of *Don Quixote*, the entire remaining manuscript was rescued from a satchel of papers destined for a junk collector in

---

[2] At several points in Part I, Cide Hamete and Cervantes are referred to as existing within the time of the characters about whom they write. Cide Hamete, in Chapter 16, is said to be a relative of the muleteer who is in the inn. Cervantes' name comes up in Chapter 6 as author of *La Galatea* and friend of the Curate. The innkeeper also alludes to the author of *Rinconete y Cortadillo* as a former guest at his inn. These suggestions of contemporaneity are undermined, however, by other indications that the authors of Part I of *Don Quixote* have to rely on archives for their source material.

a Toledo market place. Everything and everyone whose adventures the reader has before him were once contained in that satchel and buried under an incomprehensible Arabic script. It is not until the story of the *Curioso impertinente* that this situation occurs again. The manuscript of the *Curioso impertinente* has long since been left in the inn by its author in a suitcase containing some chivalric novels. The Curate is the first to be intrigued by the title and first few lines, and then Cardenio also reads and likes them. They all agree that the Curate should read the entire thing.

By the time the Curate reads this short novel to the assembled characters in the inn, he is familiar to the reader not only because of his taste for literature, but because of the agility with which his imagination can conjure up situations by which he can manipulate Don Quixote. Without a doubt he is, within Part I of Don Quixote, the character that comes closest to controlling by his artifice the entire process of the return of Don Quixote from his second *salida*. That the character who is closest to "author" of the previous "drama" of Princess Micomicona should be the one to read this story should not be surprising. The character who was called the Second Author was nothing more than an intense reader whose curiosity and imagination had re-opened the story of *Don Quixote* at the beginning of Chapter 9. And by the time the staging of the reading of the *Curioso* is reached the reader is also familiar with the importance for Cervantes of presenting not only the story in question and the author, but also his surrounding audience. This, in part, explains the discussion of chivalric novels with the inn-keeper and the comments of his wife and daughter and Maritornes. By the time the story is to be read, all the levels of susceptibility to literature of the audience have been accounted for, and all have voiced interest in participating imaginatively in a world enclosed within the porous walls of fiction.

The unpublished manuscript read to the people in the inn is the perfect analogue to the manuscript found in Chapter 9. This is the only interpolated story completely circumscribed by the written word. Anselmo, Lotario and

Camila have none of the mobility that other characters in the interpolated stories have. Their relationship to their narrator (unknown), reader and audience is fixed. None of the characters contained within the manuscript of the *Curioso impertinente* ever emerges from that framework to intermingle with the Curate, the Barber and the others who are enjoying the story, nor do any of the audience claim any previous knowledge of these characters, either through direct contact or through hearsay. This is exactly the situation from Chapter 9 on, where neither the Second Author nor the translator has had any direct contact in the past nor can have any contact in the future with the characters who appear in the manuscript of *Don Quixote*.

The question of the relationship of the *Curioso impertinente* to the rest of the novel, so often discussed in terms of thematic parallels, seems best handled by examining structural parallels between it and other works of art in the Part I of *Don Quixote*. In both the staging of the reader and audience external to the story and the staging of the characters within the story there are similarities with the Grisóstomo and Cardenio episodes. It is especially the latter that prefigures the drama of Lotario, Anselmo and Camila by introducing the drama of Fernando, Cardenio, Lucinda and Dorotea. In both previous interpolated stories the staging of the scene in which the work is presented has been given great importance. As for the interrelation between the stage from which the work is read and the stage on which the drama is portrayed, the absolute separation, seemingly unique to the *Curioso*, actually sheds more light on the reader's understanding of his relation to *Don Quixote*. For only with the *Curioso* and Chapter 9 is an entire story enclosed in paper and the written word. The other examples of the opening up of paper and books into works of art have revealed poems or letters which only point to actual characters, not enclosing them, but suggesting their extra-poetic existence. In the *Curioso* and in *Don Quixote* itself the reader's entire knowledge of a character and his world is wrapped up within the manuscript. In these various ways, it can be clearly shown that the *Curioso* does not stand alone as extraneous matter within Part I of *Don Quixote*, but offers another example of possible narrator-character relations which both heightens the illusion of historicity of the two previous interpolated stories and sharpens the reader's understanding of the purely "poetic" aspect of the entire novel.

The attitude of the unknown narrator of the *Curioso* is unambiguous, for he often inserts his agreement with the attitudes of one of the characters (e.g. "... comenzó Lotario a descuidarse con cuidado de las idas en casa de Anselmo por parecerle a él —*como es razón que parezca a todos los que fueren discretos*— que..." or "Decía él, *y decía bien,...*" [I, 33. Italics mine]). But he also often expresses disapproval and even gets to the point where he intervenes with a desperate " ¡Desdichado y mal advertido de ti, Anselmo! ¿Qué es lo que haces? ¿Qué es lo que trazas? ¿Qué es lo que ordenas?..." (I, 33). The narrator's interventions, however, go unheeded, for the characters whose story he is writing lie outside his control. Like Cide Hamete, this narrator's role is limited to telling what is going on and commenting on the action, without having any real control over the characters or their activities. The result of this apparent limitation of the power of the author is a heightened illusion of the autonomy of the characters. This is the error into which Don Quixote, along with the inn-keeper and the Second Author, has fallen. All tend to feel that the characters' will and drive and imagination are the effective moving forces in a story whose author is simply an, if not passive, at least impotent observer and narrator.

In a discussion with the Canon (I, 49), Don Quixote makes it clear that he has never questioned the reality of the characters in the chivalric novels. Most readers also recognize Don Quixote as indeed a powerful moving force from within the novel for the creation of dramas and exciting situations. Here in the *Curioso impertinente*, Don Quixote's analogue is Anselmo who, in a more deliberate way, also feels that his dramatic imagination can move the people and things around him according to his fancy. Anselmo first learns the lesson which Fernando and Don

Quixote, in different ways, must ultimately learn. All three try to recreate the world according to their imagination and succeed in inspiring the other characters surrounding them to take into their hands the formulation of counter-dramas, equally false, by which they are deceived and trapped. This process of plot and counter-plot was enacted twice in immediate anticipation of the *Curioso*. And, significantly, neither Fernando nor Don Quixote are present for the reading of this short novel. The lesson in all three cases is that no character, from within the framework of his own existence, can successfully transpose the actions of those around him to conform to a plan of his, be it motivated by madness, malice or curiosity. Just as in *Don Quixote* itself, in the *Curioso* the reader finds a story in which the narrator is apparently stripped of omniscience and the characters seem to control the very process of the story. The *Curioso* presents in capsule form the relationship of Cide Hamete to Don Quixote and anticipates in novelistic terms the later explicit discussion of the problem by Don Quixote and the Canon.

Lotario, from the beginning, sees the problem when he says, "Sin duda, imagino, o que no me conoces, o que yo no te conozco. Pero no; que bien sé que eres Anselmo, y tú sabes que yo soy Lotario; el daño está en que yo pienso que no eres el Anselmo que solías, y tú debes de haber pensado que tampoco yo soy el Lotario que debía ser..." (I, 33). On the same level of reality, two characters have appeared where there had formerly been but one: Lotario realizes that Anselmo has made of him someone that he is not and that by doing so, Anselmo has become someone else as well. But after finding his well-reasoned discourse futile, he falls into the game and agrees, for the sake of their friendship, to portray the Lotario that Anselmo has created. From this point on, the three characters, Lotario, Anselmo and Camila, are launched into a series of "plays" in which each character in turn believes himself to be the "author," successfully manipulating the actions of the other two. What each tries to do, following Anselmo's example, is to represent the artistic situation which establishes distance between author and character, without actually removing himself in distance and time and involvement from the characters whose actions he expects to control. As in the case of Fernando, Cardenio and Lucinda, the tension that this sort of situation establishes between the artificial order of the drama and the actual chaos of the real life situation is too great to allow the drama to go on uninterrupted. Even when a work is ordered so that the readers and author share a great distance from the characters, it is clear, from the construction of the whole novel, that readers and authors tend to identify themselves with the characters. It took the actual interposing of several authors and translators to remind the reader of his distance from Don Quixote and his struggle in Chapter 8. Even when the lived time of the author and audience is clearly distinct from the lived time of the characters whose story is unfolding, the inclination remains for all three — author, audience and character — to unite in a single illusion of shared time. To protect the reader from losing perspective through this very natural process of immersing himself in the story, Cervantes has carefully created fictionalized narrators, and used the other novelistic devices discussed in Chapter 1, to break the illusion. When, however, author, audience and character do in fact co-exist on the same plane of reality, sharing the same lived time and space, all three are engulfed in the impossibility of keeping "play" separate from "real life."

In just the same way as the Curate undertook the job of inventing and directing the Princess Micomicona story, Anselmo directs Lotario and plans the stage, props and general outline of the drama Lotario must then act out. The difference is that in the Curate's story, the masks, the language, and the tale told by Dorotea are so outlandish that it would be impossible for the spectators and author to confuse her acting with her real self. Don Quixote's madness allowed for a distancing which clearly separated the roles played from the "real-life" situation. In Anselmo and Lotario's case, however, no such distancing mechanism exists, and this only heightens the possibilities for confusion. Already very early in the story signs of intrigue are present: "Dijo [Anselmo] también a Camila que no dejase solo a Lotario, en tanto que él volviese. En efecto: él supo tan bien fingir la necesidad o necedad de su ausencia, que nadie pudiera entender que era fingida" (I, 33).

Another difference between Anselmo's "play" and the Curate's is that there is no temptation on the part of Dorotea to actually "become" her role. In the *Curioso*, the situation is fraught with instability. Anselmo and Lotario are similar enough in appearance, nobility and intelligence that Camila could as easily have fallen in love with the one as the other. Camila feels, furthermore, a great deal of affection for Lotario because of his friendship with Anselmo. And, for all Lotario's resistance, Camila is beautiful: "Vióse Lotario puesto en la estacada que su amigo deseaba y con el enemigo delante, que pudiera vencer con sola su hermosura a un escuadrón de caballeros armados; mirad si era razón que le temiera Lotario." Lotario is so afraid of the little distance that separates his actual desires from the artificial ones Anselmo has directed him to express, that he can only escape losing his honor by refusing the role altogether. This of course means that he must turn the game around, making himself "author" of a fictitious recount of his conversations with Camila. When Anselmo discovers that Lotario has been lying to him, inventing conversations that never took place, he forces Lotario again into the position of pretending an interest in Camila. Very quickly the pretense fuses with his real feelings, and Lotario finds himself in the position of having to falsify again to Anselmo the recount of the outcome of the "play" Anselmo had staged. In addition he must maintain a false position with respect to Camila, hiding from her the trick which he and Anselmo had originally conceived to test her honor.

This is a play in which the stakes are high for all involved. Once Camila and Lotario have turned the tables on Anselmo, making him the deceived one rather than the deceiver, it is all-important that Anselmo maintain the illusion of having complete control. This requires in Lotario and Camila a pretense of indifference towards one another which their real feelings as lovers make almost impossible to project.

The tendency for stories to generate real situations which in turn generate more stories in a process which has no necessary end has been noted as characteristic of Cervantes' art in the sections of Part I that have been treated so far. Characters, by their own interest, build something new, moving the novel forward from character to character and situation to situation. In the *Curioso* artificial and "real" situations also generate one another and grow out of one another, but at such an alarming speed and with such a limited number of characters that soon the complexity of the artifice of the entire structure eludes the grasp of any one of the characters who helped to produce it. In the Grisóstomo story, Pedro may have been initially an author, but the direction of the story eventually left him behind as it moved closer and closer to the actual appearance of Marcela. The Cardenio and Dorotea story, although circular in that the final denouement must include them, does allow the characters a respite from their direct involvement in their story. In the *Curioso*, however, the action is circular, the effects of the play directly affecting its main characters, but no distancing allows the principals time off from their involvement. Therefore deceit engenders deceit within the same stage and among the same characters who pile up one layer after another of artifice to handle each added twist to their interrelations.

Reminiscent of Cardenio's staging as spectator at the wedding of Fernando and Lucinda, Anselmo finds himself finally hidden behind the wall hangings of his own bedroom, witnessing his wife's supposedly adulterous encounter with his friend. This was originally planned by Lotario in an attempt to dishonor Camila by revealing her deceit to her husband, while continuing to conceal to her Anselmo's role in planning the play out of which everything else had grown. However, changing his mind at the last minute, Lotario agrees with Camila to produce the play Anselmo expects to see in such a way that both Camila's and Lotario's honor are restored in Anselmo's eyes. Camila is the real "author" of this most complex invention. But, though she thinks she is controlling the situation with full knowledge of her audience and main protagonists, even she is in fact being deceived as much as the others. She has never learned of her husband's original test to her honor and is therefore unaware of the artifice of Lotario when he explains the reasons for his having first approached her. Lotario, for his part, does not know quite what to expect in Camila's performance. So successful is her portrayal of the honest wife that the narrator says: "... arremetió a Lotario con la daga desenvainada, con tales muestras de querer enclavársela en el pecho que casi él estuvo en duda si aquellas demostraciones eran falsas o verdaderas..." (I, 34). The play demands absolute verisimilitude because if any hint of make believe pokes through its surface, all the characters will be in mortal danger. Unlike the Princess Micomicona play, the artificial violence of the scene is always in danger of becoming real from the point of view of each of the spectators. When Camila pretends to kill herself, even Lotario and Leonela are not sure whether they were witnessing fiction or truth.

Camila's entire performance seems to be so thoroughly conscious and controlled that everything, including Anselmo's hidden entrance and exit, is pre-arranged. However, her maid's future deceit and Anselmo's past deceit remain beyond the reach of her control and understanding, and eventually and inevitably, Lonela pulls the single loose thread by which the entire, carefully knitted fabric comes unraveled.

This story presents the greatest single attempt of the characters to control by artifice the world about them. The effort is desperate because in the success or failure of the construct lies the very survival of the characters involved. No matter how clever and how determined the participants, however, none is powerful enough to anticipate and account for all the possible actions of each of the others. In the open-ended world of Cervantes' novel, it is clear that spontaneous, onward-flowing, unplanned life is the antithesis of an art which must block things off and wall things up, subjecting them to preconceived rules and artificial limitations. The examination of the earlier interpolated stories has shown this antithesis in interaction. Here, however, artifice and spontaneity are yoked with such violence that the reader must see as fatal the error which drives characters to seek, by static pattern, to subject and control the fluid interchanges of living people in natural contact with their environment.

The *Curioso* is the one interpolated story in which the reader and listeners are kept at a clear distance from the characters in the story. The *novela* is initially presented as a work of art complete in itself. But despite all the claims that it has as a self-enclosed work, even it must suffer interruption and a delayed ending. Every other story examined so far has left the reader waiting for more. In this story, though the end is preordained and the interruption does not leave the audience really uncertain of the outcome, the reader and the audience are nonetheless forced to wait for the undoing of the elaborate interlacings of deceit while witnessing the outcome of another drama that has been festering in the mind of Don Quixote. The implication of Don Quixote's madness is, like Anselmo's, that he feels that those around him can be subjected to a preconceived pattern by means of which all their actions are governable. The result of such an idea is that the one who so feels becomes himself subject to the same manipulation that he employs. The Curate invented a play in seeming accord with Don Quixote's wishes that actually made him a tool of the Curate's inventions. However, the Curate, like Lotario and Camila, is a character on the same level of reality as Don Quixote and is therefore no more able entirely to control Don Quixote than Camila can control Anselmo through deception. It is therefore Don Quixote who suspends the denouement of the story of Lotario and Anselmo to effect an end to the drama into which the Curate and Dorotea had thrust him. By so doing he symbolically initiates the series of denouements to follow and seems indeed to have killed the "giant" tormenting Dorotea.[3] For it is not until after his deed that Dorotea's actual solution is made possible by the near-miraculous appearance of Fernando and Lucinda. Furthermore, by really destroying the inn-keeper's wine sacks, Don Quixote presents another problem unforseen by the Curate. The Curate, for his attempt to manipulate Don Quixote's return home, winds up having to pay for the unexpected twist that Don Quixote's imagination gave to the story. Don Quixote has to some extent escaped the curate's control, though not so disastrously as Leonela escaped Camila's. This victory of "life" over "art" is doubly emphasized by the fact that Don Quixote's slashing of the wine sacks successfully interrupts at its peak of deception the work of art the Curate has been reading.

On the other hand, Don Quixote's deed reveals how intertwined life and art are. For his imaginative slaying of the giant pre-figures Dorotea's actual salvation — a turn of events only recognized by the readers who can see its central role in the climax of deception, artifice and suspense around which not only Lotario, Anselmo and Camila are gathered, but also Dorotea, Cardenio and the Curate.

4. *The Captive's Tale*

The happy ending to Dorotea's and Cardenio's story follows the unhappy ending of the *Curioso*. Just as all the reconciliations among the lovers have been made, however, the inn opens its doors to yet another couple, whose strange

---

[3] Joaquín Casalduero, in *Sentido y forma del "Quijote"* (Madrid: Insula, 1966), points out in great and subtle detail the interconnections between Don Quixote's dream and the suspended novel of the *Curioso* as well as the relationship between the happy ending to Dorotea's story and Don Quixote's killing of the giant:

> En el patio de la venta están leyendo una novela, una ficción, un sueño; en su cuarto, Don Quijote, dormido, está viviendo, soñando su novela. El sueño del Caballero interrumpe el "Curioso," alejando el desenlace trágico; pero su sueño aproxima y hace posible el desenlace feliz de la historia de la princesa Micomicona.

dress and appearance portend another interesting tale. In an initial statement which almost seems to be an overt comparison of his story with the preceding interpolated story, the man grees to recount his adventures saying: "Y así, estén vuestras mercedes atentos, y oirán un discurso verdadero a quien podría ser que no llegasen los mentirosos que con curioso y pensado artificio suelen componerse" (I, 38). The Captive's story and the *Curioso* could not be more different, not only with reference to the "truth" of each, but in the manner of the telling.

If the *Curioso impertinente* represents the extreme of the use of "pensado artificio" to control the on-going motion of life, the Captive's story, following as closely as possible the vicissitudes of his life, represents the extreme of a story controlled not by artifice but by externally caused events. Like Cardenio and Dorotea, the Captive is narrator of the events of his own life. And like theirs, the general direction of his story is circular. He begins by telling of his origin, his father's wishes for him and his brothers and of his departure to fight against the Turks under Juan de Austria. Although his present appearance as narrator suggests something of the denouement towards which the events he narrates are heading, the beginning of the story and his present ignorance of the fate of his father and brothers indicate a further resolution to be looked for outside the story itself. In the *Curioso* an external resolution to the story was impossible because all the characters, both by their own actions and by their presentation to those in the inn through the written word, are trapped in deception. Here the story is told, not read, and the narrator is also the main character of his story. Therefore a potential shift in levels of fiction is built into the Captive's story, as it was in Dorotea's and Cardenio's story and as it was not in the *Curioso*. Both the content and the presentation of this story tie it to events outside itself on a plane with the Curate and all the company in the inn.

In the Captive's story, very little is staged. Seldom does the captive quote directly or allow the characters to speak and move in apparent independence of his control. Only in moments of most intensity are the characters dramatized. When the Captive narrates his first meeting with Zoraida in her father's garden, he presents her speaking in her own voice, and skilled in the use of deceit and double meaning. She is shown in an intensely personal conversation with the captive in the presence of her father, who remains ignorant of her intentions. The second scene dramatized is of Zoraida and her captive father on the boat the prisoners have bought for their escape. These two scenes, although important for the real understanding of the conflict in which the Captive and Zoraida were involved, slow down the pace of an otherwise fast-moving narrative. The Captive's story ranges over 20 years and carries him in a nearly circular journey around the Mediterranean. Many potential characters are given brief mention and passed by. Clearly the major interest of this narrative is the effect of the events narrated on the present and future lives of the Captive and Zoraida. In the *Curioso*, the ratio of narrative to staging is the reverse of that in the Captive's story. The characters in the *Curioso* are given nearly free rein by their narrator, who limits himself in time and space to the direct presentation of their deeds. This contrast between centrifugal and centripetal narrational forces is represented in the *Curioso* and the Captive's tale, respectively, and reflects the structure of the novel as a whole. Built into *Don Quixote* is a tension between contraction and expansion. In either a history or a poem, both must be present, with the balance differing with respect to the formal aspects of the art in question. Here the two approaches to the writing of a short-story are contrasted in the *Curioso* and the Captive's tale.

CHAPTER III

FICTIONAL "DRAMAS" IN PART II

1. *General Distinctions between Part I and Part II*

Part II of *Don Quixote* shows to some extent the effects of Sansón Carrasco's comment in Chapter 3, that extraneous matter marred the unity of Part I. Because of the changed nature of Don Quixote's relation to the world about him, it will be easier in Part II to relate the various interpolated stories to Don Quixote's own adventures. In Part I the creative impulse rested to a large extent in Don Quixote's hands as he enjoyed relative anonymity while seeking out his adventures and stories. The publication and wide divulgation of the story of *Don Quixote de la Mancha*, however, made Don Quixote famous by Part II and almost universally recognized as the chivalric hero of Cide Hamete's book. The result is that rather than being unaware, or taken by surprise by Don Quixote's madness, the characters whom Don Quixote meets in Part II tend to anticipate and exploit for their own entertainment his credulity. Thus such stories as Grisóstomo's, Cardenio's and the Captive's, though possible (e.g. the *bodas de Camacho*, Ricote, Roque Guinart), have not nearly the significance in Part II that they had in Part I. The major fictional authors of Part II have Don Quixote, rather than their own life-stories, as their subject. Don Quixote, now within the covers of a book, has almost entirely lost his "author" and "spectator" roles to become the subject of other characters' manipulations.

This major shift in Don Quixote's role in the novel from "author" to "character" carries with it shifts in the roles of other characters as well. In most of the stories analyzed in Part I the reader could see a development on several fictional planes. In the Grisóstomo and Cardenio stories, for example, a tale first introduced at two removes from the reader would subsequently unfold and reveal characters acting out the ending at one remove. In all but the *Curioso*, which remained enclosed within its paper manuscript, the stories shifted, from the characters' point of view, from the imaginative to the actual. Characters, first merely heard about, eventually materialized to produce before the eyes of the audience the final results of a story. In Part II the principal subject of nearly all the plots is Don Quixote. Because of this, the reader, to a large extent, has lost the privileged position from which he can see the creative process enacted. As in the *Curioso impertinente*, the deception and the real action take place simultaneously on the same stage. Nearly all the fictional authors in Part II share the time and level of reality of the characters whose actions they try to manipulate.

The result of this juxtaposition of fiction and reality is that the readers, like Don Quixote, Sancho, and the other characters, run the risk of being deceived, of having no basis on which to distinguish contrived plots from the spontaneous actions of the characters. The reader has no way of telling when the characters are acting as authors and when they serve as characters controlled by an author outside the story. Because of this possible confusion, an author beyond the characters' scope is the reader's only point of reference. Cide Hamete, only briefly and infrequently mentioned in Part I, becomes a much more salient figure in Part II as a result of the need for distancing and clarification. He appears at least a hundred times in the course of Part II to comment, to explain, or to be commented upon.

The emergence of Cide Hamete carries a further implication. Since the Moorish surrogate author is powerless to make contact with the world of the characters about whom he is writing, his appearances and comments, or the comments of his translator, are directed to and made for the benefit of the reader. The reader's role is much more clearly defined in Part II, just as Cide Hamete's role as author is more thoroughly developed. When Cide Hamete takes it upon himself to explain the truth behind the appearance after one of the characters has elaborately deceived Don Quixote, it is for the reader's appreciation. No longer is it common, as it was in Part I, for the reader to overhear a story and watch its unfolding as if he were simply another of the spectators within the book. The reader is much more consistently held at a distance from the spectators of the plots in Part II.

Just as Cide Hamete shows his distance from the activities of his characters by his increased appearance and by his awareness of the reader in Part II, the character-authors also hold Don Quixote at a great distance. In most of the stories in Part I there was a clear involvement of the character-author in the story he was telling. Most of the character-authors in Part I, in fact, were the main characters of their stories and in no way pretended any but stylistic control over their narrations, dependent for their plot upon fortune and history. Even in the *Curioso*, where each character tries by artifice to control the actions of the others, their motives for perpetrating the deception relate to their own real feelings, and the intended result of the deception is a change in their real situations. On the other hand, the machinations of the Duke and Duchess and Don Antonio, which take up a good portion of Part II, are very nearly gratuitous. What they plan for Don Quixote has no purpose beyond their own entertainment. They aspire to act as puppeteers, controlling completely Don Quixote's movements without having their own lives touched at all by his activities. This is not the only relation between character-authors and Don Quixote in Part II, of course, for Sansón Carrasco, Maese Pedro and Sancho, when they perform plays for the deception of Don Quixote, are not acting from entirely disinterested motives. Some twenty-five chapters in Part II, however, are devoted to the purely entertainment-motivated activity, wherein some characters devise plots of which they are only authors and spectators, and Don Quixote and Sancho are only characters — a clearly-marked and artificial division of roles impossible in Part I.

Don Quixote's role in Part II is not confined exclusively to his being a puppet manipulated by the will of idle, diversion-seeking characters aware of his madness. Although his energy and will to transform his surroundings into material for his own play of knight in shining armor are clearly reduced in Part II, he is still the initiator of many incidents and activities. In Part II his imagination has lost the vitality by which in Part I it transformed *ventas* into *castillos* and *labradoras* into *doncellas*. Very early in Part II this is made clear by the reversal of the roles played by him and Sancho with respect to Dulcinea. In the second *salida*, Part I, it was Sancho who remained astounded and incredulous while Don Quixote plunged himself into the task of "killing" windmills whom he had, by an act of imaginative will, transformed into giants. The enchantment of Dulcinea, however, reveals a basic change which will be characteristic of the entire second part. Neither Sancho nor Don Quixote actually sees as beautiful *doncellas* dressed in riches and riding white chargers the three donkey-riding *labradoras* whom they find along the road. But Sancho, who knows well the credulity of his master with respect to enchantments, quickly devises a "play" which he acts out with this credulity in mind. Sancho creates the entire act for the benefit of his audience, Don Quixote, and for the sake of saving himself from Don Quixote's rage. Here is the first of a series of character-authors in Part II who deceive with full awareness of their deception, inspired not by their own creative urge or convictions, but by a knowledge of their audience and the weaknesses of the people whom they intend to deceive. And here is Don Quixote, no longer projecting his vision upon the world but allowing the world to control his actions.

Not rendered completely passive, however, Don Quixote does successfully engage the *Caballero de los Espejos* in battle, challenges the lions, intervenes in the denouement of the *bodas de Camacho* episode, brings forth marvels from the depths of the *cueva de Montesinos*, seeks adventure in the *barco encantado*, jumps on Maese Pedro's stage to destroy the Moors who are in pursuit of Melisendra and Gaiferos, and offers to fight for Doña Rodríguez's daughter's honor. These adventures take the shape of Don Quixote's own will and show his ability still to escape the control of those character-authors engaged in the effort of completely taking charge over his actions.

An understanding of the *Curioso impertinente* is most instructive when considering Part II. Cide Hamete, having been criticized for allowing his pen to flow so freely in Part I as to write stories little connected with the adventures of Don Quixote and Sancho, is determined in Part II to keep his attention focused almost entirely upon his two main protagonists. The result is that the *bodas de Camacho*, the story of Ricote and Ana Fenix, and the story of Roque Guinart and Claudia Jerónima are the only episodes in which Don Quixote's appearance and response are purely peripheral to the central action. Only in these episodes are his personality and madness not considered, nor do they effect significantly the denouement. In order to follow Don Quixote's and Sancho's actions almost exclusively, Cide Hamete has had to keep the action to a large extent on a single plane, the plane on which Sancho and Don Quixote act and move.

In Part I there are many examples of characters who tell stories by which the reader can get an idea of the scope and nature of artistic control within *Don Quixote*. The two basic patterns for artistic control by characters within the story were the narrated autobiographies and the plays of deception. Of the latter type, the two most notable examples were the Fernando-Cardenio-Lucinda episode and the *Curioso impertinente*. Both, however, were enclosed within the framework of a narration or manuscript by which they were kept at two removes from the reader. Both narrated dramas in Part I were seen as examples of the way the controller can become the controlled when he tries to manipulate the actions of other characters living in his own time and place. In Part II the second type of control — control of other characters on the same plane through deception — appears not encased within a narrative framework, but on the same level as that on which Don Quixote and Sancho act. Because of this, the problem of narration is left to Cide Hamete, which partially explains his increased appearance in the novel in Part II. The role of narrator which in Part I was sometimes taken over by Cardenio or the author of the *Curioso* has now been fully assumed by Cide Hamete, making him at the same time more identifiable as author and more thoroughly a character. A clearer impression of Cide Hamete's role in the work can be obtained through a study of the character-authors in Part II and the relation of their "plays" to Cide Hamete's presentation of them.

2. *Sancho*

There are five major character-authors who interact with Don Quixote in Part II: Sancho Panza, Sansón Carrasco, the Duke and Duchess, Don Antonio, and Ginés de Pasamonte. They all try to control Don Quixote's actions by anticipating the behavior the peculiarities of his madness dictate. Taken in order of their distance from and disinterestedness in Don Quixote, the first character-author to be discussed is Sancho Panza. Though closest of all to Don Quixote, and most often character for other character-author's plays, he can, when pressed by his own needs, become himself an author in a play designed to fool Don Quixote. In the cases of the enchantment of Dulcinea, the melted cheese in Don Quixote's helmet, or his supposed self-inflicted beatings, Sancho consciously tailors appearances to Don Quixote's madness. In all three cases Sancho successfully deceives him.

Sancho's involvement with Don Quixote is too great, however, for him consistently to make an object out of Don Quixote for the purposes of manipulation. His own ambition and simplicity make him eager to accept, and be accepted, by Don Quixote. Only when threatened with loss of standing with Don Quixote does he take recourse to deception. Nor is his control over the fictitious world of Dulcinea's enchantment — his most elaborate play — perfect. The Duchess, the most accomplished fictional author of all in Part II, easily convinces him that "...el buen Sancho, pensando ser el engañador, es el engañado" (II, 33). In one second, Sancho's whole artifice collapses and Don Quixote's world view entirely re-establishes itself in his mind: "...y ahora quiero creer lo que mi amo cuenta de lo que vió en la cueva de Montesinos, donde dice que vió a la señora Dulcinea de Toboso en el mismo traje y hábito que yo dije que la había visto cuando la encanté por sólo mi gusto; y todo debió de ser al revés, como vuesa merced, señora mía, dice, porque de mi ruin ingenio no se puede ni debe presumir que fabricase en un instante tan agudo embuste..." (II, 33).

3. *Sansón Carrasco*

Of considerably greater distance from the imaginative world of Don Quixote is Sansón Carrasco, who weaves his way in and out of Don Quixote's life throughout Part II. As with the fictitious authors of Part I, Sansón is well read and "muy gran socarrón," "de condición maliciosa," and "amigo de donaires y de burlas." He is the first character in Part II whom Don Quixote meets who has read Part I. Although Sansón takes pleasure in throwing himself at Don Quixote's feet and praising him as the greatest of all knights errant, he is a friend of the niece, the housekeeper and the Curate, and is aware of their worry over Don Quixote's madness. As a student and reader, and being a natural "amigo de donaires y de burlas" he is tempted, merely for his own enjoyment, to construct plots through which Don Quixote's madness can be revealed. But as he is also a neighbor and friend, this entertainment motive is tempered by the more useful intention of saving Don Quixote from his affliction by bringing him home again once and for all. The criticisms and questions he has about *Don Quixote* Part I show that he is thoroughly familiar with

Don Quixote's madness and Sancho's simplicity, as well as with chivalric novels from which Don Quixote drew his self-portrait.

For all his awareness and enjoyment of playing the part of *Caballero de los Espejos* for Don Quixote's sake, Sansón fails in his elaborate and self-assured scheme when Don Quixote accidentally overcomes him in a duel and very nearly kills him. In several ways, as a result of this unexpected failure, Sansón reveals that he is what Sancho was more ready to admit about himself — the *burlador burlado*. Sansón had chosen Tomé Cecial, a friend of Sancho's, to be his squire in the play which they were to perform. Tomé, though an "hombre alegre y de lucios cascos," is not nearly as involved as Sansón in the literature of chivalric novels or in the interests of Don Quixote's family and friends. It is he, then, who, when faced with the possibility of continuing the deception or allowing Don Quixote to kill the disguised Sansón, rushes in to admit that all had been a play and a fraud. He shows knight and squire the plaster nose he had used as a mask and begs them to spare Sansón in his foolish ruse. In the *Curioso*, Anselmo, hidden behind the curtains watching what he thought to be the murder of his best friend and suicide of his wife, was confronted with the same problem as Tomé: to recognize at what point artifice and reality were going to join, at what point the sequence of events followed by the logic of the play would irreparably affect the irreversible sequence of events in real life. This problem presents itself whenever the play and the true situation take place on the same level of reality.

After the battle is over and Don Quixote has departed, proud and happy over his victory, it is Tomé who asks the penetrating question: "Sepamos, pues, ahora: ¿cuál es más loco: el que lo es por no poder menos, o el que lo es por su voluntad?" (II, 15). They agree that those who willingly become mad can just as willingly give it up. This, however, proves more difficult for Sansón than he would have anticipated. Tomé is very pleased to take his leave of this acting game to return home. Sansón, however, refuses, vowing to find Don Quixote again and to give him a good beating. He speaks now, not out of amusement or concern for Don Quixote, but out of anger and the desire for vengeance. The play became real for Sansón, and his mock battle a true one, once his puppet character, Don Quixote, escaped his control and defeated him in the process. Sansón has entered the world of Don Quixote's madness and has become actually involved at this juncture in what was originally only a play directed by him.

In the first battle between Don Quixote and Sansón there was no all-knowing audience for whom the action could be performed except the readers of the book. This is where the importance of Cide Hamete manifests itself. For he performs two functions: he presents the action for the reader's entertainment and then explains the deception involved in the action. Although the reader is told in Chapter 7, Part II, that Sansón had been conferring with the Curate and the Barber and had promised the housekeeper and the niece to help recover Don Quixote's sanity, the exact plans had been left unannounced, with only a mysterious "...y el Bachiller fué luego a buscar al cura, a comunicar con él lo que se dirá a su tiempo" to indicate a future attempt to deceive Don Quixote. When the actual adventure of the *Caballero de los Espejos* takes place, the reader is left uncertain as to whether this new knight is another madman or an actor. From the hint in Chapter 7 it is clear that the author who is presenting this story knows full well the truth of the incident, but that he deliberately withholds some of the information in order to control the reader's response. It is not until Don Quixote has defeated the mysterious *Caballero de los Espejos* that the author says: "¿Quién podrá decir lo que vió, sin causar admiración, maravilla y espanto a los que le oyeron? Vió, dice la historia, el rostro mismo, la misma figura, el mismo aspecto, la misma fisonomía, la misma efigie, la perspectiva misma del bachiller Sansón Carrasco" (II, 14). After all this, Cide Hamete devotes a chapter to the explanation of just how the whole deception had been carried out. This chapter, of course, is not addressed to spectators built into the book, but to the reader. The implications of this build-up, mystification, and revelation are that while Sansón believes himself to be the author and controller of Don Quixote's actions, he is also only a character in a book, of whose existence he is unaware. Just as when Sansón, in Chapter 3, spoke about a promised but as yet unpublished second part to *Don Quixote*, unaware that his very words constituted a part of that second volume, here, also, he is a character within a book, his actions and speech controlled and selected by the author for an audience of which he knows nothing.

When Sansón appears in Chapter 64 to give the death blow to Don Quixote's knightly wanderings in the guise of the *Caballero de la Blanca Luna*, the mystification which the readers underwent in the episode of the *Caballero de los Espejos* is dramatized in the conversation of Don Antonio and the Viceroy. The *Caballero de la Blanca Luna* has challenged Don Quixote on the beach. Then: "Llegóse el visorrey a don Antonio, y preguntóle paso si sabía quién era el tal Caballero de la Luna, o si era alguna burla que querían hacer a Don Quixote. Don Antonio le respondió que ni sabía quién era, ni si era de burlas ni de veras el tal desafío. Esta respuesta tuvo perplejo al visorrey en si les dejaría o no pasar adelante en la batalla..." (II, 64). Despite their conviction that Don Quixote was mad and a fit object for tricks and deceptions, there is still room for doubt, for believing in the possibility of some other knight actually engaging Don Quixote in serious battle. And just as the reader was disabused by Cide Hamete after the first battle, so Sansón clarifies the situation for Don Antonio, explaining his intentions and the reason why he appeared in such a manner.

Sansón confesses to Don Antonio that he spent three months roaming as a knight errant in search of Don Quixote in order to defeat him in battle. Yet at the end of Don Quixote's life, Sansón is one of those most enthusiastic about the idea of exchanging the chivalric for the pastoral life. Despite Sansón's confidence in his sanity and ability to control the life of Don Quixote through deception, Don Quixote succeeded in escaping his control. And perhaps more importantly, Sansón came, in the process of deceiving Don Quixote, strongly to resemble the very knight whom he believed he was controlling. Finally, while carrying out his project, Sansón remained unaware that his performance and Don Quixote's were, and still are, being enjoyed by an audience numbering in the millions and reaching hundreds of years away in time from the moment in which he believed he was living.

4. *The Duke and Duchess*

Chapters 30 to 50 of Part II are given over almost entirely to the activities and *artificios* constructed by the Duke and Duchess for their amusement and for the deception of Don Quixote and Sancho. Without doubt the Duke and Duchess are the most consummate of all the character-authors in the book and construct the most elaborate plays of all. Like other major character-authors in the novel, they are idle, literate, well-versed in chivalric novels, and, in the twist unique to Part II of the novel, they have read Part I and are well aware of Don Quixote's insanity and the possibilities for manipulating him. Since Cide Hamete has limited himself to the recounting of the adventures of Don Quixote and Sancho, nothing is known about the Duke and Duchess except that which involves them with the two major characters. All the reader knows about them is that they are idle and imaginative. It is no coincidence that these characteristics both identify them with Don Quixote and allow them to become active figures in Part II. Here we see again how Cervantes' novel generates a seemingly limitless number of characters who become characters by virtue of their penchant for imaginative engagement in the lives of others. Making the same mistake Sansón has made, the Duke and Duchess willingly enter the contrived world of a known character in a book thinking that they can remain at the same time outside of the story. All of Part II is based on the mistaken assumption, on the part of the would-be all-controlling character-authors, that they can deal with a fictional character and maintain at the same time a distance which allows them never to slip into that fictional world with which they plan to entertain themselves. Like Sansón, they are trapped from two directions: they are controlled to some extent from within their play by the very characters whom they intend to manipulate, and from without by an author of whom they are unaware, by whose will and whose hand all that they do is contrived.

Numbers of times in the plays which the Duke and Duchess have caused to be performed, the effect they have produced is powerful enough to draw them in for a moment and to elicit from them an unfeigned reaction. For example, when the Duke and Duchess prepared for the parade of evil spirits in the forest after the wild boar hunt, they arranged for trumpets and bells to resound announcing the event. When the noise actually erupted, however, it took them all by surprise with its din. "Pasmóse el duque, suspendióse la duquesa, admiróse don Quijote, tembló Sancho Panza, y finalmente, aun hasta los mismos sabidores de la causa se espantaron" (II, 34). Even the authors most thoroughly aware of the artifice can be drawn into the appearance, albeit for a short time only. Over and over again in *Don Quixote* the theme is echoed "que aun los sabedores de la burla estuvieron por creer que era verdad lo que oían" (I, 46), a theme central to the entire novel and from which even the most uninvolved and self-conscious character-authors cannot escape.

This one indication that the Duke and Duchess are susceptible to a momentary loss of distance over their spectacle is followed by other more important deviations from the planned order. Doña Rodríguez, the maid whom Sancho offended in their first encounter by asking her to take care of his donkey, has remained unaware of the atmosphere of deception surrounding the house and has managed to be so anxious to find help for her own problem that she is willing to take Don Quixote's boasts of himself at face value. In enlisting Don Quixote's aid, she upsets the order and calm with which the Duke and Duchess manage their tricks. Telling Don Quixote of her mistress' beauty secrets, she so enrages the Duchess who is listening to her from outside the door to Don Quixote's room that she causes the Duchess to break in to give both her and Don Quixote a thrashing and to escape unidentified. Neither Doña Rodríguez's credulity nor her divulgation of her mistress' secrets were in the Duchess' plans, but both demanded a response requiring of the Duke and Duchess further deception. The important point, however, is that the Duchess, when enraged, is no longer in control of the situation and becomes a character involved on the same level as Don Quixote, whom she had believed that she was controlling completely. Like Sansón, when faced with his defeat by Don Quixote, she responds not in a distanced, disinterested manner, but with involved feelings of revenge. Again, the play has transformed itself into reality, and the author has become a character.

The same thing can be seen in the Altisidora episode. Initiated by Altisidora herself, the idea was then taken up by the Duke and Duchess that after Don Quixote's song to Altisidora from his window, cats with bells tied to their tails would be thrown from the roof. "Fué tan grande el ruido de los cencerros y el maullar de los gatos, que, aunque los duques habían sido inventores de la burla, todavía les sobresaltó..." (II, 46). Again the trick escapes their control, and Don Quixote is actually hurt by the cat's scratches: "Los duques... se fueron pesarosos del mal suceso de la burla; que no creyeron que tan pesada y costosa le saliera a Don Quijote aquella aventura..." (II, 46).

In a similar way Tosilos, the lackey chosen by the Duke to fight Don Quixote in the trumped-up battle which Doña Rodríguez's impertinence forced the Duke to stage, fails to conform to the plot-line of the Duke's invention. Three times it is repeated that the Duke has instructed Tosilos well as to his role in the performance (once in Chapter 54 and twice in Chapter 56), but all is to no avail, for Tosilos breaks out of his role, despite his instructions, and falls in love with Doña Rodríguez's daughter. The Duke's scheme is unsuccessful both because his character, Tosilos, substituted his fictional role for his real feelings, and because the deceived audience discovered the fraud by which the real husband of Doña Rodríguez's daughter was replaced by Tosilos. Again it is rage and anger that break through the calm control of the Duke, turning him into a character with real feelings, a *personaje incitado*, to use Américo Castro's term. Furthermore, the Duke's illusion of control appears to be nothing but an illusion. Looking back over the chain of events that lead up to Tosilos' and Doña Rodríguez's daughter's possible marriage, it can be seen that the developments were very little affected by the Duke's will. He neither planned Doña Rodríguez's first request for help from Don Quixote, nor her further pleading at the dinner table a few days later. In the first instance the Duchess became the surprised observer of Doña Rodríguez's actions and in the second all, including the readers, are left in suspense, wondering who the two mysterious women in mourning are who enter the dining room unannounced: "... y aunque los duques pensaron que sería alguna burla que sus criados querían hacer de Don Quijote, todavía, viendo el ahinco con que la mujer suspiraba, gemía y lloraba, los tuvo dudosos y suspensos..." (II, 52). The decision to stage a battle between Don Quixote and the young man who deceived the daughter of Doña Rodríguez came about as a result of Don Quixote's decision to defend her honor, and not by some scheme previously devised by the Duke. The Duke's only real role in the whole performance of the battle is to instruct his lackey Tosilos to do his part, and to provide the stage on which the battle is to take place. But the denouement, like the beginning, escapes his control. Only much later does the reader discover that the apparent ending of the battle at Chapter 56 was not the end of the story. As Tosilos tells Don Quixote in Chapter 66, the Duke reasserted his control in the form of disciplinary action against him, and the apparently happy ending of Chapter 57 came to nothing but disappointment.

On Sancho's island, also, real feelings escape the pattern of controlled artifice set up by the Duke and Duchess for the sake of everyone's amusement. But, as in the castle, some of those on the island were not aware of the trick being played on Sancho, who provides situations not anticipated even by those who feel themselves to be in control. And again, even those who are aware of the trick are still capable of genuine reactions of amazement: "El traje, las barbas, la gordura y pequeñez del nuevo gobernador tenían admirada a toda la gente que el busilis del cuento no sabía, y aun a todos los que lo sabían, que eran muchos" (II, 45). In fact, Sancho's entire governorship is a source of surprise, not only to those characters who are *sabidores*, but to the reader as well. No one expected of Sancho the discretion with which he dispatched the problems and cases brought before him. And it is finally the mayordomo who must admit, speaking of Sancho's wisdom, "Cada día se ven cosas nuevas en el mundo: las burlas se vuelven en veras y los burladores se hallan burlados" (II, 49).

Among the various cases brought before Sancho in his rounds is one which was unplanned by the Duke's men. When the police bring before Sancho the young woman dressed as a man, the author says: "... y los consabidores de las burlas que se habían de hacer a Sancho fueron los que más se admiraron, porque aquel suceso y hallazgo no venía ordenado por ellos, y así, estaban dudosos, esperando en qué pararía el caso" (II, 49). Having become ingenuous spectators as a result of this unwarranted appearance of a beautiful young girl, the tricksters are as likely as anyone else to be taken in by her situation. The result is that the *maestresala*, so well instructed in his fictitious role with respect to "governor" Sancho, falls in love with the girl, and, breaking out of his prescribed, distanced role, spends a sleepless night, following which he intends to ask for her hand in marriage.

These are a few examples of the basic point, made over and over again on every level in the novel, that no matter how much control one character pretends to have over another and how elaborate and disinterested are the plays by which he expects to determine the actions of another character for his own entertainment, the characters never completely succumb to the control imposed on them. The "author" becomes involved, and the deceit is always in danger of being discovered by the audience. An allegory of the two ways in which the will of the character or audience eludes the will of the author can be found in two of Sancho's encounters on his island. Immediately preceding the discovery of the girl dressed up in her brother's clothes is the presentation to Sancho of a clever boy who has been caught trying to escape from the law. When Sancho, for the boy's impertinence, orders that he sleep in jail that night, the boy explains that no matter how many chains he has on or how many guards there are, the governor can never make him sleep the night in jail because no one can make him sleep if he doesn't want to. Sancho replies, "De modo que no dejaréis de dormir por otra cosa que por vuestra voluntad, y por no contravenir a la mía" (II, 49). At this, Sancho releases him. This insistence on the freedom of the character against the will of whoever would control him is basic to Cervantes' art.

In the following episode, already mentioned, of the young girl in her brother's clothes, Sancho, having heard her halting, confused story sums it up for her in the following way: "...nos salimos a espaciar de casa de nuestros padres con esta invención, sólo por curiosidad, sin otro designio alguno..." (II, 49). This is another example of a character striking for freedom against the control of another as she represents escape from control on two different levels: her father's control and the Duke's control. The *invención* by which she staged her adventure was uncovered, however, and her disguise was broken, revealing her true situation. Like the Duke and Duchess themselves, her invention represents nothing but a disinterested desire to be entertained, leading to consequences not anticipated in the original plan. She is in exactly the same situation as the Duke when Doña Rodríguez and her daughter discover that the knight opposing Don Quixote is Tosilos and not the one whom they thought. Fabrication of plots with character, author and audience on the same level always runs the risk of being uncovered, bringing on consequences reaching far beyond the initial intention.

From these examples it can be seen that the Duke and Duchess' calm certainty that they can control the events planned for Don Quixote and Sancho is an illusion. Actual feelings and real situations keep intruding on the fictitious ones, forcing them out of shape and wresting the denouements from the hands of the imitators. But the illusion of control is also undermined by the presence of Cide Hamete, who is nowhere in the novel more evident than in these episodes that center around the Duke and Duchess' castle as he, darting in and out between the chapters, demonstrates his dominion over the material.

5. *Cide Hamete*

To what extent Cide Hamete himself actually controls the story he is presenting to his readers is a question which must be taken up in detail later, for a compilation of all his appearances in the book shows that his control over his material is ambiguous. Nonetheless, he appears to comment or show his power at least to order the material he is relating no less than twenty-five times in the course of the chapters dealing with the Duke and Duchess. In the middle of one of the most complicated plays contrived by the Duke and Duchess, the author intervenes with an apostrophe to Cide Hamete's genius as historian. Trifaldi, the *dueña dolorida*, and her duennas have just revealed their hair-covered faces to the assembled, and Trifaldi, after giving a lamentation on their state, faints, or appears to faint. This ends Chapter 39. Chapter 40, however, rather than immediately continuing where the story left off, begins with an address to the reader concerning his debt to Cide Hamete for the fascinating story he is reading. Suddenly the reader is again made aware of his distance from the scene being played out in the Duke's garden. Again the reader is forced to remember that not only Don Quixote and Sancho, but also the Duke and Duchess, are characters in a book, and that their existence depends on the good will and interest with which Cide Hamete "pinta los pensamientos, descubre las imaginaciones, responde a las tácitas, aclara las dudas, resuelve los argumentos..." (II, 40). Whether Cide Hamete is actually an inventor or a historian, the reader must in any case recognize his dependence on him for whatever he knows about the characters, and realize that the Duke, whatever his pretensions, is also Cide Hamete's creature. As a result of the distancing the appearance of the author causes in the reader's involvement with the characters, it becomes clear that the reader must look upon the Duke and Duchess in the same way that the Duke and Duchess look upon Don Quixote — as novelized entities by whom he is entertained: "¡Oh autor celebérrimo! ¡Oh Don Quijote dichoso! ¡Oh Dulcinea famosa! ¡Oh Sancho Panza gracioso! Todos juntos y cada uno de por sí viváis siglos infinitos, para gusto y general pasatiempo de los vivientes" (II, 40), says the translator or Second Author, for whom, as for the reader himself, the story is first of all transmitted by means of the written word. Clearly, from this quotation, the reader is intended to consider all, including Cide Hamete, as part of the book, removed from the reader's own lived time.

Again in Chapter 44 Cide Hamete makes the reader aware of his authorship in his famous complaint about the restrictions placed on him as author of Don Quixote's and Sancho's deeds. Later in the same chapter he again calls attention to himself to expatiate on the evils of poverty. In the following chapter (Chapter 45) he invokes the favor of the sun in clarifying the "escuridad de mi ingenio" in order to continue the narration. In Chapter 48 again he interrupts the narrative to bring attention to himself, saying how much he would give to be able to see Doña Rodríguez and Don Quixote in the scene he was describing. Later, in Chapter 53, he discourses on the caprices of Fortune and finally, in Chapter 70 he explains the Duke and Duchess' final trick and gives his opinion of them. All of these interventions will be extremely important in a later consideration of Cide Hamete's role in the novel, but for the present they need only be mentioned as examples of moments when the reader is reminded that his participation with the activities is not direct, but secondary, depending on the skill and veracity of a character on another level who has been assigned the task of relating a story. All of these interventions serve further to disrupt any tendency the reader may have to credit the Duke and Duchess with genuine authorial power over the fictitious world they believe themselves to be creating.

The most important and consistent appearance of Cide Hamete in this portion of the novel is as manipulator of the two threads of the story when Don Quixote and Sancho separate during Sancho's governorship. Since there is no way smoothly to move from Sancho's adventure to Don Quixote's, if both are to be given equal time and the reader's interest is to be maintained, Cide Hamete must appear regularly to explain why one story is being interrupted and where the other story left off. By his doing so, the reader is reminded constantly of the novel-writing perspective of Cide Hamete from which all characters on the Duke and Duchess' level, despite what they may think, are simply characters. And further, the reader is made aware of Cide Hamete's role as author at least partially in control of these characters. Finally, the reader feels his distance from the story, and his separate role as reader, when Cide Hamete directs comments to him explicitly. His interventions show not only an awareness of his reading audience, but an interest in their reaction. For example, in Chapter 44, as Sancho sets off for Barataria, the author says "Deja, lector amable, ir en paz y en hora buena al buen Sancho, y espera dos fanegas de risa que te ha de causar el saber cómo se portó en su cargo, y en tanto, atiende a saber lo que le pasó a su amo aquella noche; que si con ello no rieres, por lo menos, desplegarás los labios con risa de jimia...." In this passage, the reader not only finds himself addressed, but characterized as to his response to the forthcoming narrative. Of further interest is the fact that there is a clear indication of foresight in this passage which in some ways contradicts the impression gathered at other points in the novel that Cide Hamete is simply an on-the-spot historian who reports deeds as he sees them and as they happen. That in this particular section of the novel he should appear to know ahead of time what will happen to his two protagonists further undermines the Duke and Duchess' illusion that they are initiating and carrying forth actions according to their own spontaneous impulses.

At the end of Chapter 44 still a further ramification of Cide Hamete's manifest control over the entire assemblage of characters in the novel can be seen. After Don Quixote has gone to bed, confused over Altisidora's declaration of love, the author intervenes to say "... donde le dejaremos por ahora, porque nos está llamando el gran Sancho Panza, que quiere dar principio a su famoso gobierno." Cide Hamete no longer appears to be merely following around characters who are independent of his will. Instead, by suspending their activity, he is showing that they can do nothing until he decides to set them into motion. While the reader has been following the narration of Don Quixote's difficulties with Altisidora, Sancho, it seems from this passage, has been merely waiting in the wings for his turn to perform, rather than continuing on his way as he would do were he "real." The beginning of Sancho's governorship depends on his author's will and not his own, or fortune's, or the Duke's. This same impression is maintained throughout most of the fourteen such interventions in the story by the narrator.

At the end of Chapter 48 Don Quixote has just been pinched and beaten by the mysterious phantasms after Doña Rodríguez's disclosure of the Duchess' secret and is sitting alone and confused. The author adds, "... donde le dejaremos deseoso de saber quién había sido el perverso encantador que tal le había puesto. Pero ello se dirá a su tiempo, que Sancho Panza nos llama, y el buen concierto de la historia lo pide." Here the author shows not only that Don Quixote must await his word in order to possibly disabuse himself, but that the story has its own logic and that such considerations as suspense and good order — purely literary considerations independent of the interests of the characters — determine to a large extent the manner in which passages are arranged in the novel.

In Part I, a great majority of the stories dealt with actual events in the lives of the narrators, allowing the characters therefore often to become participants in the conclusion of stories of which they were originally narrators. In Part II, however, where the majority of the character-authors use artifice and deception to stage their fictitious dramas, the conclusion must take place on a level removed from them, where Cide Hamete explains for the reader's benefit the mechanics of the drama we have witnessed. Since the character-authors in Part I generally tell true stories whose ending is unknown to them and in which they are involved, the readers are satisfied when fortune presents them with the conclusion to their stories. The character-authors in Part II, however, pretend to know the entire course of the dramas they stage, to recognize them as false, and not to be at all truly involved in the web of their fabrications. The emphasis, therefore, falls on the revelation of the mechanics and artifice by which a deceptive appearance was contrived, and the unfolding of every story comes at the moment when either the readers or the characters are disabused of their former deception. As in the *Curioso impertinente* in Part I, so long as the characters continue to exist deceived by one another, there is no real ending, and the situation remains inherently unstable. Only when all the strings by which the characters have been falsely moved have been revealed can the story actually rest completed.

Thus in Part II another of Cide Hamete's roles is to reveal to the reader the artifice used by the various character-authors in their tricks on Don Quixote. After each major episode, therefore, Cide Hamete breaks into the narrative to explain carefully, point by point, just how each deceit was perpetrated. To what extent Cide Hamete is also guilty of concealing information from the reader in order to later surprise him is a point which must be considered in some detail later. For the present it is enough to say that in this way also, Cide Hamete shows his ascendency over the character-authors and reveals all the pasteboard and papier-maché that went into their stagings, stripping them thereby of any omniscience or mysterious power.

Cide Hamete ends the chapter of the *Caballero de los Espejos* with a promise to explain exactly who this knight and his squire were. He then dedicates an entire chapter to revealing just how and why Sansón and Tomé Cecial decided to deceive Don Quixote and Sancho as they did. In Chapter 70 of Part II, Cide Hamete takes his leave of Don Quixote and Sancho in order to explain by what manner Sansón found Don Quixote and Sancho in Barcelona and how the Duke and Duchess decided to pull another trick on them after Don Quixote's defeat. After the episode of the mysterious pinching of Don Quixote and Doña Rodríguez, Cide Hamete again presents himself for an explanation of what happened (Chapter 50).

6. *Don Antonio*

Don Antonio is another of the character-authors in Part II who takes disinterested delight in fabricating adventures for the display of Don Quixote's excentricity for the general entertainment of all. Very much like the Duke and Duchess, though not so elaborate in his inventions, he is happy to serve as host to Don Quixote and Sancho and to invite all his friends to exploit his guest's madness while apparently celebrating his presence. Don Antonio's only well-prepared deception involves the enchanted head which answers any questions asked of it except concerning the thoughts of others. Although the reader is aware that Don Antonio intends to deceive Don Quixote and others of his friends and that there is a trick involved, the reader must rely on Cide Hamete to interrupt the narrative with a careful explanation in exacting detail of how the enchanted head was constructed, who supplied the voice, and how the operator was hidden. The reason Cide Hamete wishes to explain all this is "por no tener suspenso al mundo, creyendo que algún hechicero y extraordinario misterio en la tal cabeza se encerraba...." Cide Hamete, himself a *sabio encantador* as well as *verdadero historiador*, will not permit even a magic head that disclaims knowledge of the thoughts of others to presume a magic not entirely explainable by natural means.

7. *Maese Pedro*

There remains one more character-author to be considered in Part II, in many ways the most useful of all in revealing the mechanisms by which a character performs the role of author within the story. Except for Sancho, he is the only important character in Part II who has already appeared as a character in Part I. In Part II he takes the role almost exclusively of author, under the name of Maese Pedro, though eventually it is disclosed that he is the same person that appeared in Part I as Ginés de Pasamonte. He is the only professional performer in Part II. Through him the reader sees juxtaposed a manipulator highly skilled in deception and a character dependent for his survival on that skill. The other character-authors so far discussed have played an important part in the novel only with respect to Don Quixote and Sancho, whose delusions inspire an inventiveness not usually present in them. Sancho is mostly interested in his own welfare, when not "acting" for Don Quixote's sake; Sansón is a student when not trying to dissuade Don Quixote from his madness; the Duke and Duchess and Don Antonio are well-bred people of high social station when not seeking to entertain themselves with Don Quixote. In all cases it is Don Quixote, the master madman, who brings them to life, making them characters in his novel at the same time that they imagine themselves authors of his actions. But Ginés-Maese Pedro is different, for he is by profession, with or without Don Quixote's inspiration, a deceiver and entertainer. He is essentially the only independent author in the novel, the only one who manages to deceive everyone with whom he is involved. As such, he deserves special attention, for he provides the closest parallel on Don Quixote and Sancho's level to Cide Hamete's relationship to his readers, and to his author.

Although the manner in which the Maese Pedro episode is presented is in itself important for a clearer understanding of Cide Hamete's own method of deception, as George Haley has shown,[1] for the present this study will concern itself only with an assemblage of facts available on Ginés-Maese Pedro, disregarding the order in which they were revealed. In Part I Ginés was presented as a criminal on his way to jail. In fact, the guard explained his being more heavily chained than the rest by saying "... tenía aquél solo más delitos que todos los otros juntos, y ... era tan atrevido y tan grande bellaco, que, aunque le llevaban de aquella manera, no estaban seguros de él, sino que temían que se les había de huir" (I, 22). But in addition to being a criminal, it is pointed out that Ginés is a writer, and author of his own life story. As a writer he is proud ("es tan bueno [el libro] que mal año para *Lazarillo de Tormes* y para todos cuantos de aquel género se han escrito o escribieren" [I, 22]) and insistent upon the truth of all he has written ("lo que le sé decir ... es que trata verdades, y que son verdades tan lindas y tan donosas, que no puede haber mentiras que le igualen" [I, 22]). Being the story of his life, it deals strictly with what has happened up to the present. That he makes a point of saying that it cannot be finished as long as his life is not finished shows how exactly parallel he expects his life and the written version of it to be. So far, he explains, his book includes all that has happened "desde mi nacimiento hasta el punto que esta última vez me han echado en galeras." The separation between his life and his written account thereof, it seems, is nearly impossible to make.

As author of an autobiography which is constantly being written and pretends to follow all the deeds of its author to the present moment, Ginés de Pasamonte is already a unique character-author in Part I. For of his book, *La vida de Ginés de Pasamonte*, the reader and the characters in the novel know nothing but its author's praises. He is the

---

[1] "The Narrator in *Don Quixote*: Maese Pedro's Puppet Show," *Modern Language Notes*, LXXX (1965), 145-165.

sole reader of his book. Likewise he is its author and its main character. In Ginés de Pasamonte is presented the only character in the entire novel who is fully aware of the three-sided nature of one's involvement with his own life. As autobiographer he shows that he must participate as author, character, and spectator in a life which is simultaneously acted out and captured by the written word. As author of his own life he is at once Cide Hamete and Don Quixote, at once spontaneous actor moving forward in time and sedulous historian looking backward and recording his life as history. Don Quixote's very appearance on page one of his novel implied a historian who pre-existed him. Nonetheless, it is clear from Don Quixote's speeches in Chapter 2, Part I, that he believed himself to pre-exist a historian whom he assumes his deeds will necessarily attract. Don Quixote as acting character is unaware, except in a very general way, of the historian who is following him so closely, unaware that his existence is dependent upon the written account of it. Cide Hamete, on the other hand, is unaware that he is not only a chronicler, but a character within the history he is writing. The irony of Cide Hamete's appearances and protestations of truthfulness is that he is ignorant of the translator and Second Author who are free to see him as character and to comment on him. The mutual dependence of character and author, recognized at the end in Cide Hamete's famous parting speech (II, 73), is built into the working assumption of the autobiographer.

What is unique about Ginés as autobiographer, if the reader may take his word for it, is the propinquity of his deeds to his written account of them. True autobiography, biography, or history can only approach, but never achieve, simultaneity with the deeds it purports to recount. Yet Ginés de Pasamonte says "lo que está escrito es desde mi nacimiento hasta el punto que esta última vez me han echado en galeras" (I, 22). It is as difficult to imagine that an autobiographer could keep recording his most recently accomplished deeds as it seemed impossible to Don Quixote that a book had so soon been published about him. At the beginning of Chapter 3 Part II, Don Quixote is awaiting the arrival of Sansón Carrasco and more news of the book written about him. The author says "... y no se podía persuadir a que tal historia hubiese, pues aún no estaba enjuta en la cuchilla de su espada la sangre de los enemigos que había muerto, y ya querían que anduviesen en estampa sus altas caballerías." Sancho also shows his surprise at the omnipresence of their historian: "... y dice que me mientan a mí ... con otras cosas que pasamos nosotros a solas, que me hice cruces de espanto cómo las pudo saber el historiador que las escribió" (II, 2). Only for an autobiographer of Ginés de Pasamonte's type is the constant temporal and spatial presence of a historian possible. This very mystery is what makes the whole gallery of character-authors in Part II actually dupes of Cide Hamete, fooled when they thought they were fooling. Like Don Quixote and Sancho, they cannot believe that life process and recorded history can be simultaneously achieved. They therefore ignore the Don Quixote presented as living and forward-moving and take him only as he is statically represented in book form. They ignore the fact that their own lives, which they assume to be in process and forward-moving, are also being simultaneously transmuted into history and the written word. This, then, is the source of the dual error into which all the character-authors examined so far have fallen. They take Don Quixote and Sancho as characters fixed and inscribed in history, while believing themselves to be moving, changing, and capable of control. They fail to see that Don Quixote and Sancho are also moving and changing and that they themselves are also fixed and inscribed in a history. It can now be seen that the ever-shifting roles of the protagonists of Cervantes's novel from character to author to spectator are only more credible and humanly understandable representations of the actual unity of all three in each character, in the author, and in the novel, which are ultimately one. Only the irrepressible *burlador no burlado* Ginés de Pasamonte explains this unity in his concept of autobiography.

In Part II, Ginés de Pasamonte appears in disguise, a patch covering his crossed eye, as Maese Pedro, puppeteer and owner of a talking monkey. As with the case of the *Caballero de los Espejos*, the *Caballero de la Blanca Luna*, the *Cabeza Encantada*, the mysterious pursuing of Doña Rodríguez and Don Quixote, the *labrador burlador* on Sancho's island, and other episodes in Part II, this disguise temporarily hides Ginés' identity from the reader as well as from the other characters. Cide Hamete eventually lets the reader in on the secret of who Maese Pedro actually is and how his talking monkey trick works, but the characters in the novel never discover his true identity. This distinguishes Ginés from Sansón, who shared his secret with other characters in both his guises, and from Don Antonio, some of whose friends knew how the enchanted head operated, and from the Duchess, who explained to her husband how she and Altisidora had beaten and pinched Doña Rodríguez, and from the impertinent *labrador*, whom Sancho exposed as a fraud. In all these cases, Cide Hamete may have deceived and undeceived the reader at will, but the revelation of the deception always came from information that could be gathered on the level of the story itself. Cide Hamete, in other words, could still authentically present himself as historian while showing the reader the reality of a situation which formerly appeared different to him. He could simply report the behind-the-scenes whispering between characters the reader had previously been allowed to see only on stage. But Maese Pedro confides his guile to no one, for, in fact, his livelihood depends upon the fact that no one has penetrated his mask, as he is wanted by the law. Ginés, alias Maese Pedro, therefore, is the most isolated character of all, for his very freedom depends on his ability to remain "on stage" at all times. In Part I, Ginés de Pasamonte revealed himself as a character capable of the most incredible feats of *dédoublement* as author of an autobiography which was to record his actions from moment to moment. It is no wonder, then, that in Part II Cide Hamete, without any evidence to back him up except his own adjuration, which in itself requires explicating, would associate this autobiographer of Part I with Maese Pedro. For here, acted forth rather than written down, is another stupendous case of *dédoublement.* While all the other character-authors easily lose themselves in the labyrinth of fiction and reality which they have presumed to construct, and often become the *burlados* having thought themselves to be the *burladores,* Ginés maintains a lucidity in his life-or-death game of deception which never permits him to be trapped. In an ultimate sense, of course, he is trapped, for if he gives up his disguise, he is lost.

The only other character who must live a fictitious role so consistently and without respite is Don Quixote himself, who for quite different reasons also finds himself perpetually hiding Alonso Quijano behind his elaborately maintained fictional role. Here are the prototypes of the ultimate *burlado* and the supreme *burlador* meeting from time to time throughout the novel, and finally confronting each other on Maese Pedro's puppet stage. Since neither has the alternative to let down his mask, the direct confrontation in conflict between Don Quixote and Maese Pedro is one of high drama. Tomé Cecial, in Don Quixote's battle with the *Caballero de los Espejos,* could intervene, tearing off his plaster nose to reveal the fraud and try thereby to save Sansón's life. The Duke and Duchess could allow themselves genuine expressions of anger when their dramas did not go according to plan. Ginés, however, must never let escape any response other than that befitting his character Maese Pedro. His puppet stage, only a conventional form of entertainment whose inner workings were no mystery to any of his normal audience, was never intended truly to be a mask behind which his "real" character hid, for he had concourse with his audience as Maese Pedro before and even during the show, and was recognized by all as the manipulator, albeit skiful, of what were actually little plaster dolls. The average audience's reaction to Maese Pedro and his puppet show would be like the reaction of the Duke and Duchess' household help who were in on the secret of their tricks, but still admiring of the skill and perfection with which they were carried forth. Don Quixote's reaction, therefore, definitely reflects his own madness, and not Maese Pedro's willful attempt to deceive him. As George Haley has pointed out, Maese Pedro does everything, including revealing his monetary motives, to destroy the illusion of reality at the same time that he is putting on the show. Nothing special, for once, has been done for Don Quixote's benefit.

The real show, however, takes place on the puppet stage after Don Quixote's slaughter of the puppets. For here Don Quixote and Maese Pedro confront each other, each threatening the other with the destruction of his mask. Don Quixote saves himself from having to confront his own fictional existence by his old trick of blaming the *encantadores* for transforming Melisendra and Gaiferos into plaster images. And Maese Pedro defends himself by playing a heartfelt rendition of the bereft puppeteer whose only source of income has been destroyed. As a result of his act, the trickster Ginés is able to exact a large sum of money from Don Quixote and is on his way before daybreak, never to be encountered again, because "... no quiso volver a entrar en más dimes ni diretes con Don Quixote, a quien él conocía muy bien..." (II, 26). Clearly Maese Pedro has reason to fear Don Quixote, for their previous encounter when he was undisguised might eventually be remembered by Don Quixote, making the success of Maese Pedro's mask precarious.

The major point which distinguishes Maese Pedro from Don Quixote is his total consciousness of the role he is playing. Don Quixote's isolation from Alonso Quijano is unconscious, and the basic deception is on himself. Maese Pedro, on the other hand, is fully Ginés de Pasamonte at the same time that he is Maese Pedro. He is the author and main character of a play he acts out all the time, just as in Part I he showed himself to be simultaneously author and main character of a book he was writing.[2] This feat of

---

[2] The protean nature of Ginés de Pasamonte and his relation to Pedro de Urdemalas and other character-authors who represented the chamelion "darker side" of poetry is brilliantly discussed by Alban Forcione in *Cervantes, Aristotle, and the "Persiles"* (Princeton, 1970), pp. 319-337.

distancing is revealed on another level when, as Maese Pedro, he steps beind the puppet stage and delegates the words and actions of the theater to his puppets and *muchacho*. Both the puppets and the *muchacho* are obviously controlled by him, although the boy may at times branch out onto digressions of his own which Maese Pedro can only correct after the fact but never prevent. Both with the puppet show and with the talking monkey the important factor is that Maese Pedro works his art by delegating to creatures apart from himself the performance of actions and words actually master-minded and controlled by him. Thus he himself takes on the role of spectator or critic or translator while his lackeys pose as the originators of the action. This separation of actor from creator and spectator seems to be basic to the production of art or deception in *Don Quixote*. The illusion is maintained only as long as the deceived spectator assumes the action and intention to flow from the single character on stage.

Don Quixote can always be fooled because his very existence as Don Quixote in the novel depends on his inability to recognize the distance between the time of the character and the time of his author. His own assumption of the role of Don Quixote is an attempt — shown again and again to be unsuccessful — to completely transform his lived time into the fictionalized, suspended time of the characters in chivalric novels. But that his madness is only an extreme of what everyone suffers is clearly revealed by the fact that everyone at the inn is fooled by the talking monkey, as unlikely a phenomenon as that of the living puppets. Maese Pedro shows his real mastery over the minds of his audience by the very fact that his role as entertainer differs so in the two acts he customarily performs. Generally, Cide Hamete explains, Maese Pedro first gives the puppet show and then tries the trick of the talking monkey. In the puppet show he has no intention of deceiving his audience and feels free to comment on the interpreter's words during the course of the performance and to show himself as puppeteer before and after. The illusion and the reality of the show keep pace with one another, and both the puppets and their manipulator are available for observation. The static, prepared story, and the process by which it is presented, in other words, are simultaneously observable. Maese Pedro affects a total guilelessness in this puppet performance. Then, after the show is over, he does his tricks with the magic monkey. Here Maese Pedro's intention is to deceive his audience, whom he had previously treated to a straight-forward performance as obvious puppeteer. He easily deceives his whole audience now by simply hiding entirely behind the stage and devoting himself exclusively to his act.

In exactly the same way, Cide Hamete plays with his reader, sometimes letting him in on the mechanics of a deception being perpetrated before or during its presentation and other times keeping him caught in the mystery of some situation until after it is over. Examples of cases where both the machinations and the drama can be seen are Sancho's enchantment of Dulcinea, the Dueña Dolorida and Clavileño episode, and the incident in Barcelona of the pinning of the "Este es Don Quixote de la Mancha" sign to Don Quixote's back. In all these character-created events the viewpoint of the inventor of the incident could be seen. From that perspective the readers watched Don Quixote stumble inevitably into the trap set for him. In these instances, Don Quixote is rendered pure character, pure object. The reader sees him from the same distance from which the audience of Maese Pedro's puppet-show sees the puppets that dangle before them. In other incidents, however, the reader is limited to Don Quixote's point of view and shares in the process of deception with him. Some examples, already mentioned, are the episodes of the *Caballero de los Espejos* and the *Caballero de la Blanca Luna*, the pinching of Doña Rodríguez, and the *labrador burlador* on Sancho's island. Part I offers many more examples. Cide Hamete in these incidents still undeceives the reader, but not before showing him how easy, when limited to Don Quixote's perspective, it is to make the mistakes he makes.

Ginés' trick is unique. He fools everyone and escapes the inn without having had his disguise penetrated. Sceptical and gullible alike are duped by the wily Ginés. The reader, too, no matter how careful, would no doubt miss the hidden reference to Ginés in the "olvidábaseme de decir cómo el tal maese Pedro traía cubierto el ojo izquierdo," without Cide Hamete's mock confidential afterword about his patch-eyed puppeteer. As Haley has so beautifully shown, this Ginés-Maese Pedro episode clearly has an analogue in the situation of Cervantes with respect to Cide Hamete. Cervantes, like Ginés, maintains control over his characters by being lucidly conscious of himself while projecting only the mask of narrator into the work, keeping his true self, as author and critic, entirely hidden. Only when the consciousness of this *dédoublement* breaks down does loss of control result, as all the other character-authors but Ginés de Pasamonte have clearly shown in Part II. Ginés is the one character in the novel who is never caught with his guard down. The reader only knows of his disguise after the fact, having participated with the people in the inn in their deception.

Chapter IV

CIDE HAMETE: NARRATOR, CHARACTER, AND SPECTATOR

1. *Author-Character-Reader, Within and Beyond "Don Quixote"*

In all the stories discussed in Part I and the feats of *engaño* discussed in Part II, the audience's response could be considered in two ways. They either felt an admiration for the way the story or plot was constructed and brought forth, or a "suspension" in which they temporarily lost themselves in the story and allowed themselves to be moved forward within the temporal-spatial coordinates of the fiction set before them. Both reactions are equally valid, but are such that the two cannot be enjoyed simultaneously. Occasionally, even those who are forewarned of the deception can become overwhelmed with its presentation and momentarily fall under its spell, but during that moment, they trade their distance for involvement, and their detached admiration for suspension. In Part I, where a majority of the stories were told not for purposes of deception, but for entertainment of the audience and to give the character-author a chance to share his life and experiences with others, all characters in the audience could mingle the responses of admiration for the manner in which the story was told with a feeling of suspension in its intrinsic interest. The character-author himself in most cases was literally suspended, awaiting, without presuming to control, his destiny. Cardenio and Dorotea were artificially removed in time and space from the normal flow of their lives. It was from that distance that they were free to tell their histories — while the forward motion of their lives had been temporarily halted. And it was in a return to the participation in the forward motion of their lives that the ending to their stories was found. At that point, the narrative task of converting their actions into words was given over to someone else, they having lost the distance necessary to narrate a story. In the actual denouements, narrated by Cide Hamete, all the characters who had formerly been the audience for a story being told them, and thereby appreciators of the manner in which it was told, are allowed spontaneously to participate in the ending. Literary appreciation and total involvement, therefore, in these stories, can be naturally divided for the audience in the novel. Each character, according to his sensitivity, can appreciate the "literary work" set before him as well as participate in the events experienced by the main character. In Part II, however, where artificial constructs are much more common than narrated autobiographies by one of the characters, the two responses are no longer possible within the same spectator. The audience is divided ahead of time between the *sabidores* and the *ignorantes*. Although it is possible for the *sabidores* to be taken in by the artifice, and for the *ignorantes* to discover the deception, the two categories remain nonetheless essentially distinct with respect to the appreciation of a work of art.

Unlike the audience within the bounds of the novel, the reader is perpetually held at a distance which makes a continuous appreciation of the manner of presentation and involvement with the events presented necessary. The sensation of actual participation must always be an illusion, yet the involvement of the readers must always tend toward credulity. The ambiguities of Cide Hamete's role in the novel are very closely related to the dual necessity of every reader to be both involved in and yet distanced from the material he is reading.

Built into *Don Quixote* are characters who, when acting as audience, reveal various levels of sophistication and distance. There is Don Quixote himself, of course, whose madness renders him incapable of any critical distance at all. Then there is the Second Author, almost as involved in the story of *Don Quixote* as Don Quixote was in the chivalric novels he read ("esta imaginación me traía confuso y deseoso de saber real y verdaderamente toda la vida y milagros de nuestro famoso español Don Quixote de la Mancha, luz y espejo de la caballería manchega, y el primero que en nuestra edad y en estos tan calamitosos tiempos se puso al trabajo y ejercicio de las andantes armas, y al de deshacer agravios, [y] socorrer viudas..." [I, 9]). Another highly credulous character is the inn-keeper in Part I who, as Dorotea points out, lacks little "para hacer la segunda parte de Don Quixote" (I, 32). Of chivalric novels the inn-keeper says "... de mí sé decir que cuando oigo decir aquellos furibundos y terribles golpes que los caballeros pegan, que me toma gana de hacer otro tanto, y que querría estar oyéndolos noches y días" (I, 32). Nor is Part II lacking in gullible readers. The young girls in the Arcadia upon whom Don Quixote and Sancho stumble on their way from the Duke's house seem to have been taken in by the pretenses of *Don Quixote*, Part I. One of them, on seeing Don Quixote, says "¡Ay, amiga de mi alma..., y qué ventura tan grande nos ha sucedido! ¿Ves este señor que tenemos delante? Pues hágote saber que es el más valiente, y el más enamorado, y el más comedido que tiene el mundo, si no es que nos miente y nos engaña una historia que de sus hazañas anda impresa, y yo he leído" (II, 58). All of these responses reflect an involvement with the events and concerns of the main character which blots out any awareness of the words through which these events are incarnated.

On the other hand, there are those character-readers throughout *Don Quixote* who belong to the class of *sabidores*. The Curate, for example, explains away the chivalric novels to the unsophisticated inn-keeper by saying "... todo es compostura y ficción de ingenios ociosos, que los compusieron para el efeto que vos decís de entretener el tiempo..." (I, 32). Later in Part I, the Canon of Toledo states his case against belief in chivalric novels, basing his argument on the need of the intelligent reader to believe that the events he is reading could have happened. When the artifice is not well constructed, in other words, the critical reader's ability to lose himself in the work is obstructed by his scepticism when faced with obvious improbabilities. "De mí sé decir que cuando los leo, en tanto que no pongo la imaginación en pensar que son todos mentira y liviandad, me dan algún contento, pero cuando caigo en la cuenta de lo que son, doy con el mejor dellos en la pared, y aun diera con él en el fuego, si cerca o presente le tuviera, ... por ser falsos y embusteros, y fuera del trato que pide la común naturaleza ..." (I, 49). The task of the author, therefore, is to order his work in such a manner that his readers can derive pleasure both from the exercise of their analytic intelligence and their desire to lose themselves in the adventures of another.

Don Quixote is in many ways a lesson in reading. All the major characters are drawn into the story by virtue of their interest in imaginatively involving themselves in the lives of others or in ideas which carry them away from their daily routine. All the characters of any importance are authors as well. They have either written books or poetry, or told stories, or invented and acted out roles for the benefit of the other characters. In all this, the reader has the chance to see the relation between these characters' interpretive ability as readers (or spectators) and their success as authors. To the extent that a character identifies with the main character of the fictional world to which he is exposed, to that extent will he be prone to action and involvement as character in his own world. Thus Don Quixote, becoming completely drawn in by the actions and the characters in the chivalric novels he was reading, chose rather to imitate them than their authors, decking himself out in careful imitation of their garb and following their examples. The Canon, on the other hand, has responded to the interest that the problems of the author of such works inspire in him by actually writing some one hundred pages of a chivalric novel, which he even took to friends for inspection and criticism. Between these two poles fall all those many character-author-readers who place themselves at that distance as readers which allows them a certain awareness of the author and still does not inhibit a spontaneous interest in the main character. All of these find themselves, when becoming "authors," temporarily removed from the action which nonetheless eventually draws them in.

The reader, while being privileged to peer into this kaleidoscope where characters successively become spectators, authors and actors in a world seemingly of their own making, also falls subject to authorial manipulation. Unless reminded of the distance separating him from the events narrated, the reader on the outside may come to think himself involved in the magic world set before him, first identifying with the spectators, then with the actors in the drama. But the reader, too, must learn to master the balance between suspension and judgment. The many times that the narrator, Cide Hamete, addresses him directly makes it clear that the story he is telling is as much for his audience as the story Sancho tells Don Quixote is tailored to Don Quixote's peculiarities. The reader, like Sansón, the Curate, Maritornes, or the Duke and Duchess, is part of an audience, and like them, must at some level integrate all of his reading experiences into his actual life. The reader's reactions and interpretations of this book, like that of the various character-readers to their exposure to fiction, will be carried outside the book and into his daily life. That this process had already begun to take place is pointed out by Sansón when he says of Part I that it is "... tan trillada y leída y tan sabida de todo género de gente, que apenas han visto algún rocín flaco, cuando dicen: 'Allí va *Rocinante*' " (II, 3). Whatever happens on the level of the novel itself, dealing as it does with audience reaction, can be expected to reach beyond its paper walls to the level of the readers' own lives. To illustrate not only the reader's, but also the author's involvement in fiction and real life, Cervantes has characterized both within his novel.

2. Cide Hamete as Judged by his Transmitters

Cide Hamete is a character in a novel whose task it is to report the deeds of Don Quixote and Sancho Panza to an audience of readers. As with the other character-authors in *Don Quixote*, though unknown to him, he is encircled by readers who may interrupt and criticize him and whom he must please. At the same time he faces a vast array of characters and events whose reality he must try to project. As historian, he must faithfully chronicle, at a discreet distance, the on-going deeds of his main character while suppressing his awareness the end of his story. To actually follow all the deeds and thoughts and plans of Don Quixote and Sancho would be to throw everything into chaos, for such a jumble must, willy-nilly, be ordered. Yet to show the ending before its time would destroy the interest of the listeners, who are being exposed to all the adventures for the first time. To a certain extent, both the readers and the characters are dependent on Cide Hamete for the truth. Yet the very existence of the characters and the readers separate from him makes the truth impossible. The ordering necessary to entertain the audience makes the rendering of the main characters and their actions subject to the judgment and impressions of the author. And the unity of thoughts and actions that characterize one's spontaneous participation in the world cannot be transmitted in another medium without being broken into parts according to the author's discretion. Therefore, the author's personality becomes as important in the understanding of the story of Don Quixote as the other character-author's personalities were in the evaluation of their tales. Many different opinions of Cide Hamete's character are suggested during the course of the novel. All will be considered here, both singly and as a whole.

Cide Hamete makes his first appearance in the novel in Chapter 9 of Part I. The Second Author, although assured that the Arabic manuscript found in the market place at Toledo more or less corresponds to the story of Don Quixote he had been reading, is disturbed to discover that its author is a Moor, fearing that either Arabic-Spanish animosities or the supposed Moorish tendency to lie might preclude the possibility of an accurate account of Don Quixote's deeds. This unsettling discovery of the background of the author allows for the possibility of expansion of the story, inasmuch as he may be a liar, and for the possibility of his contracting the account of the glory of its hero, inasmuch as the Arabs and the Spaniards are enemies. The Second Author ends his meditations on the possible weaknesses of the author with "... y si algo bueno en ella [la historia] faltare, para mí tengo que fué por culpa del galgo de su autor, antes que por falta del sujeto." This commentary, in addition to planting in the reader's mind the suggestion of the author's willful or unwitting fallibility, places the author on a plane not only with the Second Author, but also with Don Quixote himself. It awakens a suspicion of competition between author and main character, and hints at a character greater than the book about him. It also implies ominously that it will be impossible to rely on an absolute authority through whom the true character and deeds of Don Quixote and Sancho will be brought to light.

Added to the difficulties that a possibly unreliable narrator presents, are hints, from the beginning, that valid information on Don Quixote is unavailable. In Part I, Chapter 2, before Cide Hamete is introduced by name, the narrator indicates that there are several versions of Don Quixote's story to choose from. "Autores hay que dicen que la primera aventura que le avino fué la del Puerto Lápice; otros dicen que la de los molinos de viento; pero lo que yo he podido averiguar en este caso, y lo que he hallado escrito en los anales de la Mancha...." The impression that the historian Cide Hamete has found his sources in written material, rather than in actual firsthand contact with Don Quixote is reinforced in Chapter 8 where the story stops because the author "no halló más escrito de estas hazañas de Don Quixote, de las que deja referidas." The Second Author, on finding nothing more written on Don Quixote, suggests "... que también su historia debía de ser moderna, y que, ya que no estuviese escrita, estaría en la memoria de la gente de su aldea..." (I, 9). Again at the end of Part I the work comes to an end with the absence of further source material: "Pero el autor desta historia, puesto que con curiosidad y diligencia ha buscado los hechos que Don Quixote hizo en su tercera salida, no ha podido hallar noticia de ellos, a lo menos por escrituras auténticas; sólo la fama ha guardado, en las memorias de la Mancha, que Don Quixote la tercera vez que salió de su casa fué a Zaragoza..." (I, 52). As in the case of the reference to written material in Chapter 2, there is indication of critical selection of sources, but no indication of the criteria on which the selection is based. Finally, even more tantalizing to the reader's doubts than these shady references to authentic and inauthentic written sources, there is the discovery of a lead box found in the walls of an old hermitage which was being renovated. Inside the box were found some papers on which Spanish verses in Gothic script were written dealing with more of Don Quixote's deeds, with Dulcinea, Rocinante, Sancho Panza, and even with the death and tomb of Don Quixote. This seems to be the ultimate burlesque on the authenticity of the written sources of Don Quixote's history.[1]

Despite the doubtful origins of Cide Hamete's story, his personal unreliability, and the distance promised by the musty and arcane manuscripts between his lived time and that of his character, Cide Hamete is nonetheless regularly proffered to the reader throughout the novel as a careful and precise historian. In Chapter 40, Part II, for example, the translator or Second Author interrupts the narrative to praise Cide Hamete's care as chronicler: "Real y verdaderamente, todos los que gustan de semejantes historias como ésta, deben de mostrarse agradecidos a Cide Hamete, su autor primero, por la curiosidad que tuvo en contarnos las

---

[1] The presence of this and many other of the fictional narrative devices discussed here have been shown to derive from patterns established in the chivalric novels, in an article by Daniel Eisenberg, "The Pseudo-Historicity of the Romances of Chivalry," to be published in *Quaderni Ibero-Americani*.

semínimas della, sin dejar cosa, por menuda que fuese, que no la sacase a luz distintamente. Pinta los pensamientos, descubre las imaginaciones, responde a las tácitas, aclara las dudas, resuelve los argumentos; finalmente, los átomos del más curioso deseo manifiesta." Again and again, in lesser expostulations, time is taken out to mention Cide Hamete in passing as the "puntualísimo escudriñador de los átomos desta verdadera historia...."

In addition to praising or censuring Cide Hamete for the job he has done in chronicling the deeds of Don Quixote, the translator and Second Author also serve as commentators on various aspects of the text. In their dual roles as readers and transmitters of the manuscript written by Cide Hamete, they show how all readers apply their own critical criteria to the work they are reading and, in the process, reproduce a work which is in some ways different from the original. If Cide Hamete's sources and reliability have already seemed doubtful, the presence of a translator and Second Author through whom his text must filter makes the final version of even more dubious veracity. In some cases, the translator chooses simply to omit passages of the original text: "Aquí pinta el autor todas las circunstancias de la casa de don Diego, pintándonos en ellas lo que contiene una casa de un caballero labrador y rico; pero al traductor de esta historia le pareció pasar estas y otras semejantes menudencias en silencio, porque no venían bien con el propósito principal de la historia; la cual más tiene su fuerza en la verdad que en las frías digresiones" (II, 18). His reasons relate to his sense of style and of what contributes to and what detracts from the overall unity of the work. In another place the translator or Second Author sees fit to omit a discussion on the friendship between Rocinante and Sancho's donkey: "...hay fama, por tradición de padres a hijos, que el autor desta verdadera historia hizo particulares capítulos della; mas que, por guardar la decencia y decoro que a tan heroica historia se debe, no los puso en ella..." (II, 12). Again, the omission is based on considerations of the appropriateness of a given passage with respect to the whole work.

In other passages, the translator paraphrases, rather than reproducing exactly, the words of Cide Hamete. In the well-known complaint by Cide Hamete about his boredom in limiting himself to Don Quixote and Sancho exclusively, for example, his words are not directly translated: "Dicen que en el propio original desta historia se lee que, llegando Cide Hamete a escribir este capítulo, no le tradujo su intérprete como él le había escrito, que fué un modo de queja que tuvo el moro de sí mismo..." (II, 44).[1a] In one of Cide Hamete's most revealing comments about his attitude toward his work, the reader is denied the certitude of direct contact with Cide Hamete's words. In another similar instance, however, the translator allows Cide Hamete's comment to be directly presented to the reader: "Dice el que tradujo esta grande historia del original, de la que escribió su primer autor Cide Hamete Benengeli, que llegando al capítulo de la aventura de la cueva de Montesinos, en el margen de él estaban escritas de mano del mismo Hamete estas mismas razones..." (II, 24). In both cases, the most important point is to reinforce in the reader the impression that there are several other layers of readers and transmitters between him and Don Quixote. The effect produces a sense of distance which offsets any lurking tendency to fall headlong into the imaginary world of the hero. The multilayering of reader-transmitters puts not only Don Quixote, however, but also Cide Hamete, in a perspective that strips him of his ultimate authority over his work.

A final type of intervention of the translator can be seen in his several appearances in Part II, Chapter 5. "Llegando a escribir el traductor desta historia este quinto capítulo, dice que le tiene por apócrifo, porque en él habla Sancho Panza con otro estilo del que se podía prometer de su corto ingenio, y dice cosas tan sutiles, que no tiene por posible que él las supiese; pero que no quiso dejar de traducirlo, por cumplir con lo que a su oficio debía...."

[1a] The obvious, and frequently observed ambiguities of this passage are unimportant in the present context.

Three times he intervenes in this chapter to point out the dubious nature of Sancho's speeches to Teresa. Clearly the translator's notion of his duty to his work is erratic in that in one place he feels free to omit passages which do not conform to his idea of the work's unity and in another he feels obliged to translate despite his doubts. If this is inconsistency of character, it is not very important at this level of our analysis. Far more important is simply the periodic insertion of doubts or corrections by an editorial reader built into the work.

3. *Cide Hamete as Seen by Don Quixote and Sancho*

Cide Hamete, while unaware of the deletions, interpolations, and comments upon his work by the translator and Second Author, cannot but acknowledge the criticisms which come from his characters. The nature of their observations is quite different from the comments made by the translator and Second Author. Don Quixote, the character most aware of the existence of an author through whom his deeds will be transmitted to the world, has no interest, or indeed, awareness, of his author's peculiarities of style. He is most concerned with having the book about him deal exclusively with his courage and brave deeds. Despite his constant insistence that his scribe be historically accurate, however, he has an almost uncanny awareness that his scribe is also a *sabio* who can control and direct his actions. When Sancho, in a moment of inspiration, calls Don Quixote *el Caballero de la Triste Figura*, Don Quixote explains away what he would otherwise have to call a stroke of genius on Sancho's part: "no es eso, sino que el sabio a cuyo cargo debe de estar el escribir la historia de mis hazañas le habrá parecido que será bien que yo tome algún nombre apelativo, como lo tomaban todos los caballeros pasados.... Y así, digo que el sabio ya dicho te habrá puesto en la lengua y en el pensamiento ahora que me llamases el *Caballero de la Triste Figura*..." (I, 19). Although never again so explicit, Don Quixote's numerous references to the *sabio* or *encantador* who controls his fate come very close to being references to his author. When, for example, Don Quixote's fantastic armies turn into nothing but herds of sheep he says "Como eso puede desaparecer y contrahacer aquel ladrón del sabio mi enemigo" (I, 18). After the disasterous incidents in the inn with Maritornes and the muleteer, Don Quixote explains to Sancho: "... no hay que hacer caso destas cosas de encantamiento, no hay para qué tomar cólera ni enojo con ellas; que, como son invisibles y fantásticas, no hallaremos de quién vengarnos, aunque más lo procuremos" (I, 17). For all that he has resolved to recreate the noble office of valiant knighthood, Don Quixote, of all the characters, is the one who seems to have a sense of being controlled by his fate, even as he determines to master it.

Don Quixote's first mention of his author appears in Chapter 2 of Part I. Having gathered helmet, sword, and steed together and having invented appropriate names for himself, his horse, and his lady, he considers himself enough extablished as a wandering knight to make his historian an inevitability. "¿Quién duda sino que en los venideros tiempos, cuando salga a la luz la verdadera historia de mis famosos hechos, que el sabio que los escribiere no ponga, cuando llegue a contar esta mi primera salida tan de mañana, desta manera?..." The distinction between the book Don Quixote envisions and the one which Cide Hamete has actually written, however, becomes clear immediately. For Don Quixote's projection of the novelized version of his first *salida* is a florid, conceit-filled description of the sunrise, his departure on Rocinante, and the countryside on which he begins his first sally. Cide Hamete's response is to copy down with all accuracy Don Quixote's words, and to follow them with a simple "y era la verdad que por él [el campo de Montiel] caminaba." The author clearly sees Don Quixote differently than Don Quixote sees himself, although he conforms enough to Don Quixote's expectations to be carrying out the duties of historian as expected by Don Quixote. Later in the same chapter Don Quixote addresses his projected author directly: "¡Oh tú, sabio encantador, quienquiera que seas, a quien ha de tocar el ser coronista desta peregrina historia! Ruégote que no te olvides de mi buen *Rocinante*, compañero eterno mío en todos mis caminos y carreras." For Don Quixote, there is no doubt that he will be a character in a book. Since the books on which he has modeled himself allow both for the heroism of the main character and the presence of *encantadores* over whom he has no control, his attitude toward his own responsibility for his deeds can properly be ambiguous, as this selection of quotations shows. He can comfortably accept the existence of a controlling author while still expecting that author faithfully to follow and record his actions. For him, the roles of *historiador* and *encantador* are not incompatible, but rather, basic to the imaginary world he is bringing to life.

It is not until Part II that the characters discover the actual existence of a book about them. When Sancho first expresses amazement that the author could know things "que pasamos nosotros a solas," Don Quixote says, "Yo te aseguro, Sancho, que debe de ser algún sabio encantador el autor de nuestra historia; que a los tales no se les encubre nada de lo que quieren escribir" (II, 2). True to his earlier statements, Don Quixote clearly believes in the possibility of having a scribe whom he has never seen publish a book about his deeds before "estaba enjuta en la cuchilla de su espada la sangre de los enemigos que había muerto" (II, 3). It is only when he discovers that Cide Hamete is a Moor that he begins to worry about the veracity of his book: "... desconsolole pensar que su autor era moro, según aquel nombre de Cide, y de los moros no se podía esperar verdad alguna, porque todos eran embelacadores, falsarios y quimeristas" (II, 3). The remainder of his criticisms are based on his preconceived notion of what a chivalric novel should be like. He disapproves of the attention given to the squire "puesto... que nunca hazañas de escuderos se escribieron," and to any extraneous material: "... no sé yo qué le movió al autor a valerse de novelas y cuentos ajenos, habiendo tanto que escribir en los míos.... Pues en verdad que en sólo manifestar mis pensamientos, mis suspiros, mis lágrimas, mis buenos deseos y mis acometimientos pudiera hacer un volumen mayor..." (II, 3). Because of the later complication of the apocryphal Second Part of *Don Quixote*, Don Quixote appears to lose his doubts about his author's competence. At the end of his life it is said of his will: "...el tal testimonio pedía para quitar la ocasión de que algún otro autor que Cide Hamete Benengeli le resucitase falsamente e hiciese inacabables historias de sus hazañas."

The most important other response of a character to Cide Hamete is Sancho's. Like Don Quixote, he shows himself true to his own character in his criticisms of the book about him. He is proud to be such a major figure in the book and hopes that his difficulties and sufferings will have been made clear to the reader. His corrections tend to focus on minutia, like the use of "doña" in Dulcinea's name. The thought of a Second Part to the history of his and Don Quixote's adventures inspires him to take on again his role as Don Quixote's squire, as he looks forward to having even more of his *gracias* in print. At one point, in fact, he addresses Cide Hamete directly: "Atienda ese señor moro, o lo que es, a mirar lo que hace; que yo y mi señor le daremos tanto ripio a la mano en materias de aventuras y de sucesos diferentes que pueda componer no sólo segunda parte, sino ciento" (II, 4). The implication is that the activity of the characters is the moving source of the story and that the author's only task is to copy down their deeds as they perform them.

4. *Cide Hamete as He Presents Himself*

The illusion that Cide Hamete is actually a historian dutifully following the movements of a main character over whom he has no control is further reinforced by his own comments and manner of presentation of the novelistic material. Rarely does he anticipate the outcome of an event in his own narration, usually reporting instead the conversations and the outcomes of the various adventures as they are experienced by the characters. Often he breaks out of the story, however, to give his own reaction or to complain about the difficulty of actually writing down on paper the full impact of the event as it happened or was experienced by one of the characters. For example: "¿Quién oyera el pasado razonamiento de Don Quijote que no le tuviera por persona muy cuerda y mejor intencionada?" (II, 43); or "¿Quién podrá decir lo que vió, sin causar admiración, maravilla y espanto a los que lo oyeren?" (II, 14); or "¿Con qué palabras contaré esta tan espantosa hazaña?" (II, 17); or "y así, desde encima del caballo, comenzó a decir tantos denuestos y baldones a los que a Sancho manteaban, que no es posible acertar a escribirlos" (I, 17). All of these examples tend to reinforce the impression that the event has not only an independent existence outside of the words that try to capture it, but that it is greater than the words chosen to represent it. The same impression, made many times, especially in Part I, that there is far more behind the written word than actually meets the eye, is created by showing only part of a selection of poems or letters. This was true in the case of Grisóstomo's poems, Cardenio's letters and notebook, and the narrative of the Captive's tale: "...y si no fuera porque el tiempo no da lugar, yo dijera ahora algo de lo que este soldado hizo, que fuera parte para entreteneros y admiraros harto mejor que con el cuento de mi historia" (I, 40).

Besides breaking into the narrative to complain of the difficulties of transforming actually experienced sensations into written words, Cide Hamete also appears as historian to lament the restrictions that sticking to a single story imposes on him. In the well-known interruption made in Part II, Chapter 44, the reader is told that Cide Hamete feels tied to "los estrechos límites de la narración," because he must include in his story only those episodes "nacidos de los mismos sucesos que la verdad ofrece." The basis of the complaint, however, seems to be connected not so much to his boredom in writing such a story as to envy, a sentiment of which both Don Quixote and the Second Author had accused Cide Hamete. For Cide Hamete is thoroughly a character, as well as a historian, and hopes to be admired for his skill as much as Don Quixote is admired for his *locura* and Sancho for his *gracias*. Thus he fears, as the translator tells us, "que muchos, llevados de la atención que piden las hazañas de Don Quijote, no la darían a las novelas, y pasarían por ellas, o con prisa, o con enfado, sin advertir la gala y artificio que en sí contienen, el cual se mostraba bien al descubierto, cuando por sí solas, sin arrimarse a las locuras de Don Quijote, ni a las sandeces de Sancho, salieran a luz..." (II, 44). Despite this complaint, Cide Hamete manages to maintain the illusion that he is, however reluctantly, a careful historian. His tendencies to expand on a story, suggested by the Second Author as characteristic of "los de aquella nación," may have been yielded to in Part I, but in Part II he gives his word that they have been checked.

Cide Hamete also seems aware, in Part II, of the possibility that his readers and characters will distrust his word. Many times he delays the beginning of a story to assure the reader that whatever may appear to be the case, the story he is about to present is true. "Llegando el autor desta grande historia a contar lo que en este capítulo cuenta, dice que quisiera pasarle en silencio, temeroso de que no había de ser creído.... Finalmente, aunque con este miedo y recelo, las escribió de la misma manera que él las hizo, sin añadir ni quitar a la historia un átomo de la verdad, sin dársela nada por las objeciones que podían ponerle de mentiroso..." (II, 10). Just before his exposé on the real identity of Maese Pedro, he even goes to the point of saying "juro como católico cristiano," which, for all of its ambiguity, reinforces the impression that Cide Hamete hopes to be believed, knowing that nothing in either the story or his character supports his credit. Equally ambiguous is his request, at the end of Part I, that the highly dubious papers found in the lead box and reconverted from Gothic script, those, that is, which were legible, be accepted by his readers. The author here is referred to as "fidedigno," and we are told: "El cual autor no pide a los que la leyeren... sino que le den el mismo crédito que suelen dar los discretos a los libros de caballerías, que tan válidos andan por el mundo..." (I, 52).

If Don Quixote can simultaneously accept his author as *sabio* and *historiador,* and the translator and Second Author can praise Cide Hamete for his truthful account while accusing him of untrustworthiness, so can Cide Hamete sustain an inconsistent attitude toward himself. For Cide Hamete, the prototype of the author, is necessarily both limited and omniscient, both a liar and a teller of truths, both dependent on his characters and free to control them. Shifting of point of view is the means that Cervantes must use for this portrayal of the ambiguous relationship of an author to his work. Richard Predmore cites numerous examples of not only the characters' confusions in interpreting the world about them, but the narrator's frequent recourse to such expressions as "parecía" and "mostraba ser" when describing a scene.[2] The effect is to make the narrator appear to be subject to the same uncertainties in interpreting reality as his characters and to place him on a plane very similar to theirs with respect to the reality he is describing. E. C. Riley has also pointed out examples of Cide Hamete's seemingly limited viewpoint with respect to particular episodes which he must describe. Riley shows at the same time, however, how frequently Cide Hamete frees himself from these apparent restrictions to demonstrate an omniscience through which the whole scene is open to him.[3]

Norman Friedman, in an article cited in Chapter I of this study, outlines eight ways that the author could control his work, moving from what he calls "Editorial Omniscience" to "the Camera," that is, from obvious authorial control to the position of a totally unobtrusive and nonselective author.[4] Of the eight ways discussed, each of which is intended by Friedman to be considered exclusive of all the others, *Don Quixote* could be said to conform

---

[2] Richard L. Predmore, *The World of Don Quixote,* Cambridge, Mass.: The Harvard University Press, 1967.

[3] Riley, *Cervantes' Theory of the Novel,* Oxford: Clarendon Press, 1962.

[4] "Point of View in Fiction," *PMLA,* LXX (December, 1955), 1160-1184.

to five. Cide Hamete intrudes with extraneous comments and moralizes on the deeds of his characters, which are the traits of a work in which "Editorial Omniscience" has been used. He also shows the traits of "Neutral Omniscience" by rendering scenes reflecting his own, rather than his characters' viewpoints. On the other hand, he could be characterized as falling into the " 'I' as Witness" category since he qualifies as a character within the story who speaks to the reader in the first person. Since his own life is at least to some extent important in the novel, he could perhaps also be considered under the " 'I' as Protagonist" category. Finally, since *Don Quixote* often gives the illusion of being self-propelled, the novel could possibly be called the "Multiple Selective Omniscience" type, in which the story comes ostensibly directly through the minds of the characters. Clearly the vacillation in identifying the exact role of the author is at the heart of the ambiguity of *Don Quixote*.

It has been shown that Cide Hamete insists upon his role as historian and often writes in a way which suggests that he is subject to the limitations of a historian or simple scribe. There are many devices, however, by which he also displays his omniscience and control over the world about which he writes. Essentially, the problem is that Cide Hamete must direct himself both toward his characters and toward his readers. This double direction of the author's concern is reflected by his exposure to criticism by both the characters and the readers within the novel. When attempting to fulfill the demands of the characters he seems most fully to be a scribe, subject to their will. This is Sancho's attitude toward his relationship to his author. When attending to the demands for interest and clarity made by his readers, however, Cide Hamete seems to be in total control. The best examples of this concern for the reader are Cide Hamete's careful explanations of the exact manner in which each of the *engaños* in Part II was perpetrated. There is no apparent way that Cide Hamete would have access to the information that Maese Pedro was actually Ginés de Pasamonte, or to how the *cabeza encantada* trick was performed. But Cide Hamete's concern lest the reader be left deceived seems reason enough for him to trade his limited view for an omniscient one. "El cual quiso Cide Hamete Benengeli declarar luego, por no tener suspenso al mundo, creyendo que algún hechicero y extraordinario misterio en la tal cabeza se encerraba..." (II, 62).

Omniscience and concern for the reader seem also to be combined in other ways. In Part II the reader is frequently addressed in such a way that the consciousness of the book as book is re-established, and the author's control over his characters is made evident. This can be seen especially well in the chapters in which Don Quixote and Sancho are separated, as was pointed out in Chapter 3 of this study. In these chapters Cide Hamete shows his control by arbitrarily stopping a story in order to continue the unfinished remains of another: "Pero ello se dirá a su tiempo, que Sancho Panza nos llama, y el buen concierto de la historia lo pide" (I, 48). Yet his control seems based primarily on a sense of proportion and ordering rather than on anything inherent in the story itself. Such considerations reflect awareness and concern for the readers as opposed to concern about the characters. Another way in which Cide Hamete makes the reader aware of himself as reader is to refer back to previous chapters or ahead to future ones. These references tend to reinforce in the reader his sense of the book as book and thereby his role in the work as reader and not as participant. Some examples are: "Puesto, pues, Don Quijote en mitad del camino (*como os he dicho*)..." (II, 58 italics mine); or "dejémoslos pasar nosotros (*como dejamos pasar otras cosas*)..." (II, 54 italics mine); or "...lo que se dirá en el siguiente capítulo" (I, 19); or "...donde les sucedió lo que se contará en el capítulo venidero." *Don Quixote* is filled with such examples, but these will suffice to show that Cide Hamete regularly redirects his attention from characters to readers and that in so doing he calls attention to himself as author and controller of a book, and as far more than the mere anonymous scribe of the deeds of others.

In the *Retablo de Maese Pedro*, the interpreter has frequent recourse to expressions such as "vean vuesas mercedes allí," and "vuelvan vuesas mercedes los ojos..." Since there is an audience which actually sees the puppets on the stage, these locutions are understandable. Cide Hamete, however, uses the same expressions at times when he is addressing no one but the reader. Once in Chapter 41 and twice in Chapter 52, there appear such expressions as "...veis aquí a deshora entrar..." from Cide Hamete. This similarity of exhortation only serves to reinforce the sensation of Cide Hamete's intermediary role in *Don Quixote*. George Haley has pointed out [5] that the interpreter's stance and role in the puppet show is as mediator between the puppets and the audience. That Cide Hamete's role with respect to the whole work is similar to that of the interpreter with respect to the puppet show is made more clear by Cide Hamete's reiteration of the interpreter's characteristic manners of speech. The parallels between Cide Hamete and the interpreter in Maese Pedro's puppet show are many, but the important thing here is to see how Cide Hamete's interventions deflate his characters' pretentions to reality, reducing them to a level not dissimilar to the puppets whose actions the interpreter points out.

Maese Pedro's puppet show was based on a well-known legend. The audience, with the exception of Don Quixote, therefore, must have been aware of the ending to the story they were watching even as they were involving themselves in its process. The audience can only involve themselves in the story to the extent that they suspend their awareness of the end. Yet their awareness of the end can serve to temper their involvement and prevent them from breaking into the magic circle of fiction with responses like Don Quixote's. Since the story of Don Quixote's adventures is unknown to the readers, Cide Hamete serves the function of detaching the reader from total involvement in the process of the story by anticipating the end from time to time. Such comments as "veis aquí a deshora entrar por la

---

[5] "The Narrator in *Don Quixote*: Maese Pedro's Puppet Show," *Modern Language Notes*, LXXX (1965), 145-165.

puerta de la gran sala dos mujeres (*como después pareció*)..." (II, 52); or "Venía en el coche, *como después se supo*, una señora vizcaína..." (I, 8); or "...no pensaba él sino en *lo que agora diré*" (II, 56 all italics mine), reflect Cide Hamete's awareness of the end of the story. Perhaps most glaring is Cide Hamete's foremention of Don Quixote's death, in Chapter 24, Part II. Examples are plentiful of Cide Hamete's references to future events. These references serve a purpose similar to that of performing a well-known tale. They again cause the reader to be aware of the distance that separates him from the time lived by the characters.

In all these instances of authorial intrusion, the intent, whether explicit or implicit, has been to reawaken the raeder's consciousness to the difference between his lived time and the time of the characters in the book. It is to cause the reader to avoid the error that Don Quixote has made that Cide Hamete appears so often in the book. That Cide Hamete sometimes allows his readers to share the *suspensión* of the *ignorantes* before disabusing them is another aspect of what could well be considered the lesson in reading that *Don Quixote* provides.

Cide Hamete, in addition to being *historiador* and *sabio*, which are aspects of his role as author, is also a character. He reveals himself as character whenever he or any of the other readers or characters in the novel refer to ideas or actions not directly related to the history he is writing. Perhaps the most personal reference to Cide Hamete's extraliterary life appears in Part I, Chapter 16. There it is pointed out that Cide Hamete knows the muleteer in the inn and is even perhaps a relative of his. Cide Hamete's personal relation to one of the characters in the novel, makes him thoroughly a part of their world. Other comments referring to Cide Hamete's Moorish background have already been discussed.

A much more common way for Cide Hamete's personality to penetrate the work is for him to explode into diatribes of his own which correspond to his state of mind rather than to the actions of the characters. When Sancho gives up his governorship, Cide Hamete comments: "Pensar que en esta vida las cosas de ella han de durar siempre en un estado es pensar en lo excusado; antes parece que ella anda todo en redondo, digo, a la redonda..." (II, 53). The miserable state of Don Quixote's socks extracts another commentary from Cide Hamete: "Aquí exclamó Benengeli, y escribiendo, dijo: 'Oh pobreza, pobreza.... Yo, aunque moro, bien sé, por la comunicación que he tenido con cristianos, que la santidad consiste en la caridad, humildad, fe, obediencia y pobreza; pero, con todo eso, digo que ha de tener mucho de Dios el que viniere a contentar con ser pobre.... Miserable del bien nacido que va dando pistos a su honra...!'" (II, 44). The speech is totally gratuitous with respect to the task of presenting Don Quixote's story to his readers, but, spontaneous as it seems to be, it is also revealing of Cide Hamete's own character. The reader is reminded of Don Quixote's similar outburst of unrelated information in Part I when he heard Cardenio refer to *Amadís de Gaula*. A small element in another story touches off a reaction in the listener which reveals his own preoccupations. In Chapter 18 of Part II, Cide Hamete appears for another expression of his own beliefs. Don Lorenzo, although doubting Don Quixote's sanity, is pleased with Don Quixote's approbation of his poetry. This causes Cide Hamete to exclaim: "¡Oh fuerza de la adulación, a cuánto te extiendes, y cuán dilatados límites son los de tu juridición agradable!..." These examples suffice to show that Cide Hamete is a character with interests outside the realm of the story he is telling.

An even more startling implication of Cide Hamete's intrusion into the novel to express personal beliefs is that he, too, is a spectator in the story of Don Quixote's life. All the above-mentioned passages result from Cide Hamete's own reaction to the story he is telling. Like all readers, he can be distracted from the course of the story by a particular point that relates to his own situation. Cide Hamete's responses as reader can be even more clearly seen in instances where his spontaneous comments relate more directly to the story itself. For example, when telling of the story of Doña Rodríguez's timid appearance in Don Quixote's room, the translator explains: "Aquí hace Cide Hamete un paréntesis, y dice que por Mahoma que diera por ver ir a los dos así asidos y trabados desde la puerta al lecho la mejor almalafa de dos que tiene" (II, 48). In addition to revealing a personal detail about his own life, Cide Hamete shows here that he has let himself become thoroughly involved in his story. In another instance, he gives a great laudatory speech to Don Quixote: " ¡Oh fuerte y sobre todo encarecimiento animoso Don Quijote de la Mancha, espejo donde se pueden mirar todos los valientes del mundo, segundo y nuevo don Manuel de León que fue gloria y honra de los españoles caballeros! ..." (II, 17). Momentarily, at least, Cide Hamete has lost himself in his character, the very reaction that much of the novel is calculated to prevent. After explaining the engineering of the Duke and Duchess' last trick on Don Quixote and Sancho, Cide Hamete adds his own reaction: "y dice más Cide Hamete: que tiene para sí ser tan locos los burladores como los burlados, y que no estaban los duques dos dedos de parecer tontos, pues tanto ahinco ponían en burlarse de dos tontos" (II, 70). In all these cases, and many more, Cide Hamete reveals that aspect which always constitutes a character in a work: he shows, in the instances mentioned, a loss of distance. As has been seen again and again throughout this story, there is a direct correlation between loss of distance and loss of control. Every character-author in the novel became a character at the point at which he lost the sense of distance which held him apart from the work he was producing. Cide Hamete, as can be seen from the quotations above, has not escaped that tendency and therefore has not succeeded in maintaining absolute control over his novelistic world.

Like the other character-authors in *Don Quixote*, Cide Hamete's role shifts from character to author to spectator. However, unlike the other character-authors, he has no potential contact with the world he is describing. Though he may at times address Don Quixote directly, as the author in the *Curioso* addressed Lotario directly, his words have no effect nor are they heard by Don Quixote. For as author and historian, Cide Hamete must necessarily live in a future time, from Don Quixote's point of view (thus *sabio*), and from his own point of view he must see all of Don Quixote's actions as past. Although this awareness of the end distinguishes Cide Hamete from his readers and allows him control over their responses, he also must participate in the readers' view in order to capture their interest. One of the major lessons throughout the study of the character-authors in *Don Quixote* is that the narrator can never isolate himself from his audience, but must gear his narration to their interests. The result is that Cide Hamete must stage great portions of the story of Don Quixote and his adventures as if he, too, were following them for the first time, just as Cardenio, from his distanced position, would tell the climax of his story as if he were involved in it again, following it through from beginning to end. The *burladores* in Part II, in order to make their *engaños* effective, must appear to trade their over-all vision for the naive vision of uninitiated spectators. For the purpose both of participating with, and of controlling his audience, therefore, Cide Hamete must leave his vantage-point at the end of Don Quixote's life and enter into its process, reducing his role in many cases to scribe. At times, however, when rendering Don Quixote's life in process, Cide Hamete, too, becomes lost in the story. Like the other character-authors analyzed in *Don Quixote*, Cide Hamete shows his lack of total control by his failure always to maintain a distance from the work he is creating.

Cide Hamete's activity and the activities of his characters, though analogous, are exactly reversed in the creating of the novel. While a character is narrating a story, Cide Hamete limits his work to simply writing down what is said, following the words of the narrating character who has achieved enough distance to tell others of his past. When this narrating character falls back into the flow of his life, Cide Hamete must re-establish his distance from the scene and carry it forward by his own abilities to condense and order experience. The movement, therefore, from spectator to author, which so often occurs within the story, is recapitulated on Cide Hamete's level in a reverse parallel with his characters.

In the case of the series of tricks played on Don Quixote in Part II, Cide Hamete's task is more difficult, for the artistry of the characters is not verbal, but staged, and therefore must be described by Cide Hamete, rather than simply copied down. Complicating his task further, the events he must describe are at the same time adventures of great wonder for Don Quixote and feats of artistic control for others of the characters. Cide Hamete must choose in his description of any given *burla* whether imaginatively to associate himself and his readers with the event as it happens to Don Quixote, or with the character-author who pretends to control him. Whichever approach he chooses, he must then, as with the narrated stories, re-establish his own over-view for the purpose of moving the story forward. As has been shown, none of the characters who invent situations for the manipulation of Don Quixote can maintain control indefinitely, since the distance necessary for the production of a work of art cannot long be sustained by a character sharing the same time and space with his subjects. Since in the case of the *burlas* the sharing of the character's point of view requires that he immerse himself in the characters' trickery, Cide Hamete re-establishes control when he explains to his readers the secret behind the deception. This is why Cide Hamete so often appears after a major deception (*Caballero de los Espejos*, *Caballero de la Blanca Luna*, Maese Pedro, *muerte de Altisidora, la Cabeza Encantada*) to indicate in detail to the readers the method by which it was engineered.

As historian and story teller, Cide Hamete must at the same time be controlled by the past, focusing as accurately as is possible on his characters, and actively control the past, organizing it with an eye to the reader. The complexity of the novel is increased by the fact that Cide Hamete is not only a conscious author, but also a character. Through his own extra-narrative comments about himself and the criticisms and comments of the translator and second author, the reader is allowed to see Cide Hamete outside his author's role. At times, Cide Hamete loses his sense of control over the story that he is telling, as does the narrator in the *Curioso* and also the interpreter in Maese Pedro's puppet show, and enters in with exclamations of his own. In the same way Don Quixote, as sure as Cide Hamete usually is of his ability artificially to control his universe, suspects an *encantador* of controlling him. Since both are characters, limited forever by their very roles to different levels of fiction, their comments on and suspicions about each other can only be confused and tentative.

Only Ginés de Pasamonte solves the problem and maintains complete objectivity while participating subjectively. He, however, not so much solves it as says he does. The magnificent tantalizing autobiography he speaks of in Part I is never produced; the reader is only awakened to the possibility of such by his comments. In Part II, on the other hand, he manages an act of total deception by keeping his real self at two removes from his audience, showing them only his stage and the mask of Maese Pedro, behind which Ginés himself remains permanently concealed. In the perfect work of art in which the present can be viewed both as in process and past at one time, either the work or the artist must be absent. In Part I, Ginés presents the theory but not the work; in Part II he presents the work but not himself. Clearly, for Cervantes, a work can appear to be a self-enclosed, self-sufficient entity only if it has an author built into it. But equally clearly, any built-in author must also be a character, and therefore fallible.

BIBLIOGRAPHY

1. Avalle-Arce, J. B. "Conocimiento y vida en Cervantes," *Deslindes Cervantinos*. Madrid, 1961.
2. ———. "El curioso y el capitán," *Deslindes Cervantinos*. Madrid, 1966.
3. ———. *La novela pastoril española*. Madrid, 1959.
4. ———. "Don Quijote, o la vida como obra de arte," *Cuadernos hispanoamericanos* (1970).
5. ———. "Don Quijote," *Suma cervantina*. London, 1973.
6. Battaillon, Marcel. "Relaciones literarias," *Suma cervantina*. London, 1973.
7. Casalduero, Joaquín. *Sentido y forma del "Quijote"*. Madrid, 1966.
8. ———. "La lectura de *El curioso impertinente*," *Homenaje a Rodríguez-Moñino*, I. Madrid, 1966, pp. 83-90.
9. Castro, Américo. *El pensamiento de Cervantes*. Madrid, 1925.
10. ———. *Cervantes y los casticismos españoles*. Madrid, Barcelona, 1966.
11. ———. "Los prólogos al *Quijote*," *Hacia Cervantes*. Madrid, 1967.
12. Durán, Manuel. *La ambigüedad en el "Quijote."* Mexico, 1961.
13. Eisenberg, Daniel. "The Pseudo-Historicity of the Romances of Chivalry," *Quaderni Ibero-Americani*.
14. Forcione, Alban. *Cervantes, Aristotle, and the "Persiles."* Princeton, 1970.
15. Friedman, Norman. "Point of View in Fiction," *PMLA*, LXX (December, 1955), 1160-1184.
16. Girard, René. *Mensonge romantique et vérité romanesque*. Paris, 1961.
17. Haley, George. "The Narrator in *Don Quixote*: Maese Pedro's Puppet Show," *Modern Language Notes*, LXXX (1965), 145-165.
18. Immerwahr, R. "Structural Symmetry in the Episodic Narratives of *Don Quixote*, Part One," *Comparative Literature* X (1958), 121-135.
19. Locke, F. W. "El sabio encantador: The Author of *Don Quixote*," *Symposium*, XXIII (1969), 46-61.
20. Marías, Julián. "La pertinencia del Curioso impertinente," *Obras completas*, III. Madrid, 1959.

21. Montesinos, José F. "Cervantes, antinovelista," *Nueva Revista de Filología Hispánica*, VII (1954), 499-514.
22. Predmore, Richard L. *The World of Don Quixote*. Cambridge, Mass., 1967.
23. Riley, E. C. *Cervantes's Theory of the Novel*. Oxford, 1962.
24. ———. "Episodio, novela y aventura en *Don Quijote*," *Anales cervantinos* V (1955-56), pp. 209-230.
25. ———. "*Don Quijote*," *Suma cervantina*. London, 1973.
26. ———. "Narrative Points of View in *Don Quixote*," MLA Speech (unpublished), 1965.
27. Riquer, Martín de. "Cervantes y la caballeresca," *Suma cervantina*. London, 1973.
28. Romberg, Bertil. *Studies in the Narrative Technique of the First Person Novel*. Stockholm, 1962.
29. Spitzer, Leo. "Linguistic Perspectivism in the *Don Quixote*," *Linguistics and Literary History: Essays in Stylistics*. Princeton, 1948.
30. Sterne, Lawrence. *Tristam Shandy*.
31. Unamuno, Miguel de. *Vida de don Quijote y Sancho*. Madrid, 1938.
32. Wardropper, Bruce. "The Pertinence of the *Curioso impertinente*," *PMLA*, LXXII (1957), 587-600.
33. Willis, Raymond. *The Phantom Chapters of the Quixote*. New York, 1953.

www.ingramcontent.com/pod-product-compliance
Lightning Source LLC
Chambersburg PA
CBHW030657230426
43665CB00011B/1133